WITHIN REASON

A GUIDE TO
NON-DEDUCTIVE REASONING

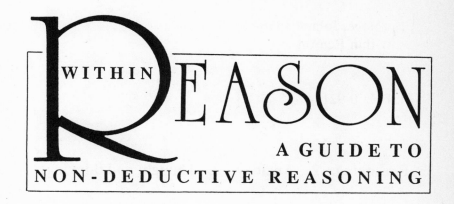

WITHIN REASON

A GUIDE TO
NON-DEDUCTIVE REASONING

JOHN BURBIDGE

broadview press

Cataloguing in Publication Data

Burbidge, John, 1936-
  Within Reason

ISBN   0-921149-55-7

1. Reasoning. 2. Analogy. 3. Thought and thinking.
I. Title

BC177.B87 1990   160   C90-093408-5

Printed in Canada on acid free paper.
Copyright © 1990, Broadview Press Ltd.

broadview press   broadview press
P.O. Box 1243   269 Portage Rd.
Peterborough, Ontario   Lewiston, NY
K9J 7H5   Canada   14092   USA
(705)743-8990   (705)743-8990

ACKNOWLEDGEMENTS

This book started from discussions with Jerry Larock, a student in Philosophy 105 at Trent University, and has benefited from the reactions of other students in the course to a preliminary draft. Bruce Wardhaugh, David Gallop, and Trudy Govier have read parts of the text and made comments. Barbara Burbidge has gone over the whole with an eye to readability. My thanks to all.

Selections on pages 57, 60/61, and 93, from *Fragmented Gods*, copyright © 1987 Reginald W. Bibby, are reprinted with the permission of Stoddart Publishing Company Limited. Other permissions to reproduce copyright material are indicated at the point where the material is used.

CONTENTS

INTRODUCTION

Books on reasoning and argument frequently concentrate on deduction. They spell out the forms that make a categorical syllogism valid, or the truth tables that establish a propositional argument. In both, we learn to provide neat rules that make it easy to decide whether an argument is good or not.

If, instead, they focus on induction, there is a similar narrowness of attention. Because generalizations from a sample frequently involve percentages and statistics, the discussion moves into theoretical mathematics, with discussions of probability, calculation of accuracy and controlling for variables.

Seldom, however, do people reason using statistical generalization or deductive forms like *modus ponens*. Much more commonly they begin with certain beliefs which they hold to be true, then move to others that they think follow. And this psychological process carries with it varying degrees of reliability.

Recently much attention has been paid to this more informal kind of reasoning, and books have been written on the subject. But because there are no clear rules for success, it has been easier to identify the way people go wrong than to talk about ways the arguments could be improved. Different kinds of fallacies are listed, and psychologists are encouraged to investigate why the mistakes might have occurred in the way they did.

When we turn to the texts that have moulded our Western tradition, and look there for the reasons used to support their claims, we seldom find neat patterns. Yet these works have acquired their influence because they present a reasoning that is persuasive. If there are fallacies they are not obvious; whenever one scholar claims he has found an error in the logic, other scholars soon emerge to show that the mistake was in the limited perspective of the critic, not in the original text.

A student trained in the traditional discussions of logic, formal and informal, has few resources with which to assess this kind of reasoning. At some stage in their arguments, authors may assume that we know how to use the standard syllogisms, and give us only one premise, leaving us to provide the rest. But the main thrust of their reasoning relies on much less formal and precise forms. And while these writers seldom commit outright fallacies, some of their arguments are stronger and more convincing than others.

This book is concerned with just these less formal and precise forms of reasoning. It suggests criteria of assessment for distinguishing weak arguments from strong. While it discusses induction and correlations, it leaves aside technical material concerning probability, and concentrates on the basic inferences involved.

Running through this approach is a single theme. H.W. Fowler, in *A Dictionary of Modern English Usage*, writes that "analogy is perhaps the basis of most human conclusions, its liability to error being compensated for by the frequency with which it is the only form of reasoning available."

Analogy is here taken as a fundamental motif in human reasoning. Not only is it frequently used as the major premise in a simple argument from analogy, but it also is the foundation for generalizations and inductions. As well, inferences to explanation and to action frequently appeal to analogies in reaching their conclusions. Over and over again, we find people working from "the presumption that things whose likeness in certain respects is known will also be found alike or should be treated as alike, in respects about which knowledge is limited to one of them." (Fowler again)

By identifying some criteria to be used in assessing analogies, we will have a basis for evaluating some more complicated forms of non-deductive inference.

However, not all reasoning can fit these frameworks. And so the book concludes with a discussion of arguments that do not conform to the standard molds. Even though no specific criteria of assessment can be stipulated for these inferences, it is still possible to evaluate how success-ful they are in establishing their conclusions.

Because it focuses on non-deductive reasoning, this book does not attempt to cover all the material usually considered in courses on critical thinking or informal logic. However, it does presuppose familiarity with some of those skills: how to standardize arguments, whether to accept premises as true or reliable, what are the basic patterns of deductive reasoning. Since some users of this work will not have this background, the balance of this introduction will provide an outline of what is required.

STANDARD FORM

Reasoning, inference and argument are several names for the same thing. It involves a sequence of connected thought that moves from some beliefs to others. Some ideas thus provide a basis for adopting or believing a claim.

For example, we started the last paragraph in the pre-vious section with a sentence that read: "Because it focuses on non-deductive reasoning, this book does not attempt to cover all the material usually considered in courses on critical thinking or informal logic." The "because" clause qualifies the main clause of the sentence by suggesting *why it is the case*.

The important point here is the connection between those two clauses. The one introduced by "because" provides the basis for the other, which is thereby derived from it. The former offers a *reason* for the latter. And when reasons are set down in this way to answer the question: *why is such and such the case?* we have what is formally called an argument. The reasons we call *premises*, the result we call a *conclusion*. So "this book focuses on non-deductive reasoning" is the premise of an argument; "it does not attempt to cover the usual material" is the conclusion.

Not all sets of beliefs and claims are expressed as arguments. People may simply state a belief; then go on simply to say the same thing in other words, trying to help others understand just what they are saying. They are not thereby providing reasons for believing it to be true.

At other times, someone will give a description or tell a story, outlining a number of events or characteristics that are simultaneous or in sequence. Even though there may be a connection between the thoughts, it is a connection of space and time, not a connection of reasoning.

Inference (or the relation between premises and conclusions which we call "arguments") is the focus of our interest in this work. We can identify passages that contain arguments whenever we notice that some claims are answering the question *why* — that is, why should we believe another claim to be true?

The terms we frequently use in answering the question *why* will also signal a likely premise in the writings of others: "because..."; "for..."; "since...". There are also other words frequently used for indicating a conclusion: "therefore..."; "so..."; "thus..."; and "hence..."

Whenever we want to figure out whether an argument is a good one or not—whether the reasoning is strong or weak—we need to "set out" the premises and the conclusion. We call this *standardizing the argument*. It involves listing the premises and placing them before the conclusion:

> **Premise 1:** This book focuses on non-deductive reasoning.
> **Conclusion:** It does not cover all the material usually considered in courses on critical thinking or informal logic.

Since there are frequently two or more premises, we number them. (There may be more than one conclusion, but that does not often happen.)

Standardizing can become more complicated. After all, the premises may also need some support. So they become conclusions in turn, with their own premises. We call these *sub-arguments*; since we will want to get them clearly defined in order to assess them as well, we build them into our standard form:

> **1P1:** There are many books on deductive logic.
> **1P2:** Other books talk about argument structure and fallacies.
> **Premise 1:** This book focuses on non-deductive reasoning. [**Sub-conclusion**]
> **Conclusion:** It does not attempt to cover all the material usually considered in courses on critical thinking or informal logic.

Notice that I have added an extra indent to the premises of the sub-argument, so that we will not become confused concerning which premises lead to which conclusion.

In this elaborated argument, we have added some reasons for our original premise about focusing on non-deductive reasoning and fitted them into our standard form.

RELIABLE PREMISES

Since premises are to provide reasons for believing the conclusion, they will do their job only if they themselves deserve to be believed. In other words, an argument will not be convincing if we know the reasons supporting the conclusion are either false or highly unlikely. If instead they are uncertain possibilities, the conclusion of our argument cannot be expected to be any more reliable than they are.

Therefore, before there is any point in asking whether the premises provide good reasons for believing the conclusion, we need to look at the premises on their own. Are they true, or at least highly likely to be true? Do they describe things we know from our own experience, or from the experience of people we can trust? If they express a value judgement, is that judgement widely shared? Or are we quite uncertain about their reliability? Do we have reasons for thinking they are false or highly controversial?

In answering those questions we must rely on our own judgement — what we know and have experienced. If we do want to use help from other people or outside sources, we should have strong assurance that they are dependable and that they know what they are talking about. After all, if an argument is being used to convince us, we need to be sure that its foundation is trustworthy. Since there are no neat rules to decide such questions, it is a good idea to be cautious and develop our own skills of critical judgement.

DEDUCTIVE REASONING

In some arguments, true premises *require* true conclusions. We call them deductions. And while it is not our
purpose in this book to investigate deductive reasoning,
some of the basic forms are sufficiently common that they
are often simply mentioned or assumed. For readers who
do not have a background in either categorical or propositional deduction, we shall review some of their forms, and
at the same time warn against others that seem deductive,
but in fact are not.

We shall look at arguments that are deductive simply
because of their form or pattern.

(Many deductions hinge on the meanings of the words
used: "Since John is behind Mary, and Susan is ahead of
Mary, then Susan is ahead of John." The deductive inference here relies on the meaning of "behind" and "ahead
of". Many arguments that are not deductive because of
their form are nonetheless deductive because of their
meaning. In these cases, to decide whether the meaning of
the premises *requires* a particular conclusion involves a
careful consideration of what is involved in the meaning of
the terms used. Since there are no rules that can be applied
to these kinds of deductions, it is not easy to develop a
theoretical structure for handling them. As a result, attention is usually paid to the inferences that are deductive in
form. And that is what we shall do here.)

HYPOTHETICAL ARGUMENTS

Several of the most familiar forms of deductive reasoning
are based on hypothetical judgements: sentences that have
a clause that begins with "if" or "whenever". "If the Blue
Jays are to win the pennant, they must win all their remaining games." We call the "if..." clause the antecedent, and

the main clause the consequent. (Notice that "antecedent" is a grammatical term, not a temporal one. We are not saying that the Blue Jays need to win the pennant before they win all their remaining games. It is that the "if..." clause is asserted as a condition that *logically* precedes the main clause, which it conditions.)

Whenever we have a hypothetical judgement, and can then assert independently that the antecedent is true or reliable, we have the premises for a deductive argument: "The Blue Jays did win the pennant, so they won all their remaining games." The conclusion, introduced by "so", can now state the consequent independently as well. (Notice: when we take a conditional clause and remove the conditional element we may have to shift the form of the verb as well from being conditional to being indicative.)

This form is called *modus ponens* or *affirming the antecedent*. We can represent it by substituting letters for the clauses:

Premise 1: If A, then B.
Premise 2: A.
Conclusion: So B.
}
     DEDUCTIVE

Whenever we have an argument which matches this particular pattern we know that its premises require and justify the conclusion.

Similarly, an argument is deductive when we have a hypothetical judgement together with a statement that either denies the consequent, or asserts its opposite. "The Blue Jays have lost one of their games, so they cannot win the pennant." The conclusion this time is the opposite of the antecedent.

This argument, called *modus tollens* or *denying the consequent*, has the following pattern:

Premise 1: If A, then B. ⎫
Premise 2: Not B.   ⎬   **DEDUCTIVE**
Conclusion: So not A. ⎭

One needs to be careful, however, that an argument with a hypothetical premise follows one of these two forms. For there are two arguments that look very similar, but are not in fact deductive.

One of them involves denying the antecedent: "The Blue Jays have not won the pennant, so they must have lost one of their games." This does not follow *necessarily* from the premises. The Blue Jays could have won all their remaining games and still lost the pennant if some of their opponents had won enough games to stay in front. In this pattern:

Premise 1: If A, then B. ⎫
Premise 2: Not A.   ⎬   **NOT DEDUCTIVE**
Conclusion: Not B.   ⎭

While these premises may give us *some* reasons for believing that the consequent may be true independently, they do not *require* it. The argument is not strictly deductive.

The second misleading form involves affirming the consequent: "The Blue Jays have won all their games, so they must have won the pennant."

Premise 1: If A, then B. ⎫
Premise 2: B.   ⎬   **NOT DEDUCTIVE**
Conclusion: A.   ⎭

Once again the conclusion does not follow *necessarily*

from the premises, even though they provide some support for it.

On occasion we say "If A then B" when we mean: "Whenever A happens B happens and whenever B happens A happens". In this case, the *meaning* may justify inferring to a conclusion on the basis of denying the antecedent or affirming the consequent. But we need to be sure that the reciprocal meaning is intended. In this case the argument is valid not because of its form, but because of its (unexpressed) meaning.

DISJUNCTIVE ARGUMENTS

Another deductive argument is based on a disjunctive judgement — one that says "Either Harry will go to the store or he will go to the game." The problem here is that we use "or" to say two different things. We can mean: "Either Harry will go to the store or he will go to the game, but not both." Or we can mean: "Harry will do at least one or the other, and he might do both."

Because of this ambiguity in meaning, there is only one form of disjunctive argument that is deductive: "Harry did not go to the game, so he must have gone to the store."

Premise 1: Either A or B.
Premise 2: Not B.   **DEDUCTIVE**
Conclusion: So A.

(The second premise could be "Not A", in which case the conclusion is "B": "Harry did not go to the store so he went to the game.")

Since at least one is to be done, the fact the second is ruled out makes the first mandatory.

A related argument is not deductive in terms of its form, however. Simply because Harry *did* go to the store we cannot conclude that he did not go to the game.

Premise 1: Either A or B.
Premise 2: A. } **NOT DEDUCTIVE**
Conclusion: So not B.

For that argument to work, we need to be sure that "either... or..." *means* "not both". If it might mean "at least one" then the conclusion is not required. Because the meaning of the phrase has to be considered before a decision can be reached, the inference is not deductive in terms of its form.

CATEGORICAL ARGUMENTS

A final set of deductive inferences works from sentences that connect two nouns or adjectives by forms of the verb "to be": "is" or "are". "Kangaroos are marsupials." "No trespassers are permitted." There are a number of these that are deductive, and an even greater number that are not. For our purposes we need mention only three.

The first one works with two affirmative statements: "Kangaroos are marsupials. All marsupials are animals that carry their undeveloped young in pouches. So kangaroos are animals that carry their young in pouches."

We can represent it this way:

Premise 1: A's are B.
Premise 2: All B's are C. } **DEDUCTIVE**
Conclusion: So A's are C.

The important point here is that the subject of the

second premise (B) must include *all* of the things named by the noun or category. It must refer to the complete class of B's. A, which serves as the subject term in the first premise and the conclusion, can be either *all*, or only *some*; but it must be the same in both places.

Once again the form is important. For an argument that sounds rather similar but has a different form is not deductive: "Kangaroos are marsupials. All animals that carry their undeveloped young in pouches are marsupials. So kangaroos are animals that carry their young in pouches."

Premise 1: A's are B.
Premise 2: All C's are B.
Conclusion: So A's are C.
} **NOT DEDUCTIVE**

By a simple device we can see that this will not work. We take an argument *with the same form*, give it true premises and show that a false conclusion follows: "Kangaroos are marsupials. All opossums are marsupials. So kangaroos are opossums." *When we can use a form to create a bad argument — one in which a false conclusion comes from true premises — we know that the argument form is not deductive.*

The second kind of categorical argument that is deductive uses one negative premise: "Poachers are trespassers. No trespassers are permitted. So poachers are not permitted."

Premise 1: A's are B.
Premise 2: No B's are C.
Conclusion: So A's are not C.
} **DEDUCTIVE**

There are several things to be careful about in this

form. Whenever we have a negative premise, the conclusion must also be negative. As in the positive argument, if all A's are mentioned in the premise then no A's are C in the conclusion; if only some A's are B, then only some A's are not C. In this form, however, it is possible to reverse the order in the second premise and keep the argument deductive.

We have only touched the surface of deductive reasoning. There are many other forms of argument in which the premises require the conclusions. However, the five mentioned here are commonly used in defending positions and justifying claims. And they are regularly assumed as components in non-deductive reasoning. Some familiarity with them, then, will be useful for understanding the pages that follow.

CHAPTER 1

ANALOGY

Early in the nineteenth century there was a great deal of interest in animals and plants. A few scientists had suggested that some species developed from others — that there was a kind of evolution. But this did not command much agreement. For there was nothing that explained how a species could change over time.

For a while, some thought that parents could pass on through their genes what they had learned from experience. For example, once a rabbit had found that a hole provided protection, its young would instinctively start to dig holes.

But scientists were never able to prove that this actually happened. No experimental evidence confirmed the hypothesis.

The young Charles Darwin, observing nature from the decks of the *Beagle*, discovered that the same species of a plant or animal developed differently in various parts of the world. But he went further. He found a satisfactory way of explaining how evolution could take place. He did this by comparing processes in nature with the methods used by breeders of domestic animals:

Man can and does select the variations given him by nature, and thus accumulates them in any desired manner. He thus adapts animals and plants for his own benefit or pleasure.... It is certain that he can

largely influence the character of a breed by selecting, in each successive generation, individual differences so slight as to be inappreciable except by
an educated eye. This unconscious process of selection has been the great agency in the formation of
the most distinct and useful domestic breeds.

There is no reason why the principles which have
acted so efficiently under domestication should not
have acted under nature. In the survival of favoured
individuals and races, during the constantly recur-
rent Struggle for Existence, we see a powerful and
everacting form of Selection. [*The Origin of Species*]

Darwin compared nature to a breeder of new animals
or plants. In a similar way, she "selected" those cattle or
roses that fitted her purposes and made sure that they
would reproduce. To describe this process he coined the
phrase "natural selection".

For the moment we are interested in the reasoning that
Darwin used in making this move. We cannot, of course,
get into his mind and follow his thoughts. But we can note
the result, and identify the pattern.

Darwin drew an analogy.

An analogy does two things. First, it expresses an
agreement or similarity. In this case, Darwin compared the
natural history of various species with the activity of
developing new plants or animals by selective breeding. He
noticed, for the first time, that they are alike.

But an analogy does more than state a similarity. If two
things are alike in all important respects except location in
time and space we call them identical, and we call their
relationship an identity. But an analogy is distinguished
from an identity in that it considers the similar features of
two things *which nonetheless are not identical*, but are in
other ways quite different from each other.

For all that I have used the pronoun "she" to refer to nature a few paragraphs back, nature is not a person with a clear sense of intention and technical means of achieving her ends. Nature is not a "thing" at all. We use the word to suggest the biological forces that encourage survival and reproduction. But these forces do not *select*. There is no deliberate choice, nothing picked out.

Darwin's analogy not only remarked on a similarity, but also indicated that the natural processes would be different from the breeder's methods. By connecting the adjective "natural" with the noun "selection" he signalled that the process of determining which species perish and which thrive occurs without the active intervention of a breeder. When we attach a modifier ("natural") to a noun ("selection"), the modifier changes the normal meaning of the word it modifies, as long as the two words are used together. In this way Darwin implied that the two processes are quite different, for all their similarity.

Much creative human reasoning uses analogy. We think of two different things at the same time, noticing that there is something similar about them. That similarity catches our interest, and sheds new light on what we are thinking about.

Darwin was not the first to think this way. His predecessors had also relied on an analogy. They thought that acquired characteristics, like learning to burrow a hole, could be transmitted in the same way that size, hair colouring, and sex are transmitted: through the genes. The difference between Darwin and those who went before him was not in the way they were reasoning, but the kind of analogy they drew.

Consider another example. In Buddhism, one of the most potent symbols is the lotus flower, which grows up from the muck at the bottom of a pond to blossom in the free air. Much is included in what the Buddhists call the

"Lotus of the Wonderful Law", or *Lotus Sutra*. But one level of meaning is easy to grasp. The lotus offers an analogy for the life of Buddha. Just as he rose above the bog of earthly desires that cause the sickness and death of our daily existence into the enlightenment of nirvana, so this flower blooms unstained by the mud from which it springs.

In one sense there are no things less similar than a water flower and the dispassionate life of an enlightened monk. Despite their great differences, however, Buddhism stresses their similarity. Indeed, the point it makes in the analogy is all the clearer because the differences are so great. The similarity stands alone.

The first point to notice about an analogy, then, is that it expresses the *similarity* of *different* things. It is the similarity that is expressly stated. We are expected to recognize the differences. But we soon discover that the unexpressed differences are equally important. They have not forgotten, even if they have not been mentioned.

There is, however, a second important feature to note about analogies. The word itself comes from Greek, and its original meaning was related to mathematics. It referred to proportions or ratios. In arithmetic, for example, we may say that 2 is to 4 as 6 is to 12. This is a proportion, or ratio. Certainly 2 is not the same as 6, nor is 4 identical with 12. What is being stated in the proportion is something else. It is the *relation between* the 2 and 4 that is the same as the *relation between* the 6 and 12. In other words, 2 is half of 4, and 6 is half of 12.

Relations are difficult things to handle in thought. We use nouns to name things. We use adjectives to describe qualities. Relations are as common as things and qualities. Yet while we have words for some of them (like "between", "father", "marries"), our language is not rich enough to cover them all.

We use analogy to enrich our language. Whenever we want to indicate and clarify a particular relation, we compare it with something else which has the same relation.

Consider the two examples we have mentioned. Darwin's "selection" connects a surviving species with an extinct species and with the need to satisfy certain constraints. That whole network of relationships is expressed in the analogy. By focusing on that network, he was able to show that evolution was a plausible hypothesis.

In a similar way, the lotus points to the contrast between our dark origins and the effortless culmination in "light" of a properly disciplined life. That relationship finds more adequate expression in the analogy than through a thousand pages of explanation.

There are, then, two features about analogies that are important. In the first place they express similarities between different things. In the second place, because the similarities are similarities of relation, we use analogies to identify relationships for which we have no normal names.

It is both of these features that make analogies so useful in reasoning. By comparing things which are normally not associated with each other, an analogy extends the range of our thoughts, and makes it possible to think of things in a new way. What it brings to our attention is a particular relation which, because it has no name in our language, had previously escaped our notice. Analogy is one of the most widespread tools we use in our thinking to venture into new areas.

EXERCISE:

For each of the following analogies identify the similarity that is expressed and the key differences that are assumed.

Then express the analogy as a proportion, so that the different terms of the one relationship are clearly parallel.

> EXAMPLE: "Suppose two people are looking at a picture or political scene. One says 'Excellent' or 'Beautiful' or 'Divine'; the other says 'I don't see it'. He means he doesn't see the beauty. And this reminds us of how we felt the theist accuses the atheist of blindness and the atheist accuses the theist of seeing what isn't there. And yet surely each sees what the other sees. It isn't that one can see part of the picture which the other cannot see. So the difference is in a sense not one as to the fact." John Wisdom, "Gods."

Similarity: One person "sees" and another doesn't.

Difference: Seeing beauty in a picture or excellence in a political scene is not the same as believing that God is present and active in the world. The first two are acts of judgment about aesthetic value or political appropriateness; the third looks for a reason or cause behind the phenomena of the world.

Proportion: The person who says "Beautiful picture" **is to** the person who says "I don't see it" **as** the person who says "God is acting in the world" **is to** the person who says there is nothing beyond the world.

1. Governing a country is like running a household in that you have to balance the budget and prevent attackers from breaking in.

2. Human beings are like machines; when you put in a stimulus you get an automatic response.

3. An atom is like the planetary system; just as the planets revolve around the sun, electrons circulate around the nucleus.

4. "The human understanding is like a false mirror, which, receiving rays irregularly, distorts and discolors the nature of things by mingling its own nature with it." F. Bacon, *The New Organon*.

5. "With what can we compare the kingdom of God, or what parable shall we use for it? It is like a grain of mustard seed, which, when sown upon the ground, is the smallest of all the seeds on earth; yet when it is sown it grows up and becomes the greatest of all shrubs, and puts forth large branches, so that the birds of the air can make nests in it." Jesus, in Mark 5:30-32.

6. "The way of advance for truth is in general the same as the way of advance for existing life: of two alternatives, one dies out, not because the other destroys it directly, but because it is less fitted to survive." J. Huxley, *Man in the Modern World*.

7. "Just as the symmetry of the human body is the result of the disposition of the members of the body, so in a State it is ordained by nature that these two classes (capital and labor) should exist in harmony and agreement, and should, as it were, fit into one another, so as to maintain the equilibrium of the body politic. Each requires the other; capital cannot do without labor, nor labor without capital." Pope Leo XIII *Rerum Novarum*.

8. "In a pot in a paint shop, along with other paints, a particular pigment serves in its entirety as so much saleable matter. Spread over a canvas, with other paints around it,

it represents, on the contrary, a feature in a picture, and performs a spiritual function. Just so, I maintain, does a given undivided portion of experience, taken in one context of associates, play the part of a knower, of a state of mind, of 'consciousness'; while in a different context the same undivided bit of experience plays the part of a thing known, of an objective 'content'. In a word, in one group it figures as a thought, in another group as a thing." W. James, "Does Consciousness Exist?"

9. "Sexual experiences, like the experiences of driving automobiles, render us liable to special moral situations. As drivers we must guard against infantile desires for revenge and excitement. As lovers, we must guard against cruelty and betrayal, for we know that sexual experiences provide special opportunities for each. We drive soberly because, before we get into a car, we believe that, except in morally unusual circumstances, it is wrong to be careless of life. We resist temptations to adultery because we believe it wrong to betray trust, whether it is a parent, a sexual partner, or a political colleague who is betrayed. As lovers and drivers, we act on principles which are particular applications of general moral principles." Sara Ruddick, "On Sexual Morality," from *Moral Problems: A Collection of Philosophical Essays*, by J. Rachel. Copyright © 1971, 1975 by J. Rachel. Reprinted by permission of Harper & Row Publishers Inc.

10. "Certainly engineers stretch, twist, compress and batter bits of metal until they collapse, but it is just by such tests that they determine the strains which the metal will withstand. In somewhat the same way, philosophical arguments bring out the logical powers of the ideas under investigation, by fixing the precise forms of logical mishan-

dling under which they refuse to work." G. Ryle, "Philosophical Arguments."

11. "When a body is once in motion, it moveth, unless something else hinder it, eternally; and whatsoever hindereth it, cannot in an instant, but in time, and by degrees, quite extinguish it, and as we see on the water, though the wind cease, the waves give not over rolling for a long time after: so also it happeneth in that motion, which is made in the internal parts of man, then, when he sees, dreams, &c. For after the object is removed, or the eye shut, we still retain an image of the thing seen, though more obscure than when we see it. And this is it, the Latins call *imagination*, from the image made in seeing." T. Hobbes, *Leviathan*.

12. "The notion that there is something of the same nature as human mind in lifeless matter at first sight appears incredible or ridiculous. Let us, however, illustrate its possibility by considering certain well-established biological facts concerning electricity. Apart from lightning, the only powerful electric phenomena known before the late eighteenth century were the electric shocks produced by the electric eel, the electric ray, and one or two other kinds of fish. The production of electricity by life might justly have appeared as something rare and sporadic. However, as physiology progressed, it was found that electric currents pass when a nerve is stimulated, when a muscle contracts, when a gland secretes; in fact, we now know that all vital activities, of whatever kind, from conscious thought to the fertilization of the egg, are accompanied by some electrical activity. The electrical charges are extremely minute and can be detected only by the most refined instruments; but they are always there. They are there because what we call electricity is one aspect of all matter.

"In the electric eel, certain muscles have been modified so that, though they have lost their original function of contraction, their electrical discharges are accumulated as in a galvanic pile, and the total voltage and current are quite respectable. Whereas in the great majority of cases the electrical properties of living matter play no special part in the life of the animal, they have become the specific function of the eel's electric organ: an accident of nature has become biologically significant.

"One may suggest that the same sort of thing has happened with mind. All the activities of the world-stuff are accompanied by mental as well as by material happenings; in most cases, however, the mental happenings are at such a low level of intensity that we cannot detect them; we may perhaps call them 'psychoid' happenings, to emphasize their difference in intensity and quality from our own psychical or mental activities. In those organs that we call brains, however, the psychoid activities are, in some way, made to reinforce each other until, as is clearly the case in higher animals, they reach a high level of intensity; and they are the dominant and specific function of the brain of man." J. Huxley, *Man in the Modern World.*

CHAPTER 2

ARGUMENT FROM ANALOGY

One of the most famous arguments for the existence of God is the argument from design. David Hume, an eighteenth century Scot, placed a particularly vivid form of the argument in the mouth of a character, named Cleanthes, in his *Dialogues Concerning Natural Religion*:

> Look around the world: Contemplate the whole and every part of it: You will find it to be nothing but one great machine, subdivided into an infinite number of lesser machines, which again admit of subdivisions, to a degree beyond what human senses and faculties can trace and explain. All these various machines, and even their most minute parts, are adjusted to each other with an accuracy, which ravishes into admiration all men, who have ever contemplated them. The curious adapting of means to ends, throughout all nature, resembles exactly, though it much exceeds, the productions of human contrivance; of human design, thought, wisdom, and intelligence. Since therefore the effects resemble each other, we are led to infer, by all the rules of analogy, that the causes also resemble; and that the Author of nature is somewhat similar to the mind of man; though possessed of much larger faculties, proportioned to the grandeur of the work, which he has executed.

As Cleanthes says, this argument involves an analogy. But the structure is more complicated than the simple use of analogy to make a point, which we discussed in the previous section.

The analogy itself is quite clear. In the division into parts and sub-parts and the adaptation of part to part, the universe resembles nothing more than a machine. For all their differences, they are alike in the way parts are related to each other and to the whole. This is the analogy.

But Cleanthes does not stop there. He goes on to point out that a machine has an intelligent maker who designs and contrives its complex structure; it does not just pop into existence. From this he draws the conclusion that the cause of the universe is "somewhat similar to the mind of man."

This passage contains an argument in that it uses two premises to support a conclusion. The first premise spells out the similarities of two different things, and thus draws the analogy between them. In the second premise Cleanthes reminds us that one of the things compared in the analogy has another feature, not previously mentioned: it has a maker. He concludes that the other thing being compared also has this additional feature.

We can standardise the argument this way:

Premise 1: The universe and a machine are similar in that both are divided into an intricate pattern of parts and sub-parts.
Premise 2: A machine has a maker.
Conclusion: Therefore, the universe has a maker.

This argument has a form which we find repeated in other, similar arguments. We shall represent the form in the following way:

— the subject of the conclusion we call the Primary Subject (PS);

— what is said about that subject is its Targetted Predicate (TP);

— the thing with which it is compared, which appears in both premises, is the Analogue (A);

— the features that connect the primary subject and the analogue in the first premise or analogy are the Similarities (S).

Using this vocabulary the argument form becomes:

P1: The Primary Subject is similar to the Analogue in ways 1 to n.
P2: The Analogue has the Targetted Predicate.
C: So the Primary Subject has the Targetted Predicate.

And we can represent the argument form in this way:
Premise 1: PS is like A in $S^1...S^n$.
Premise 2: A has TP.
Conclusion: So, PS has TP.

It is important to get this structure right when analyzing an argument from analogy. It sets the stage for assessing the argument, and for seeing how good its reasoning is — whether it provides strong grounds for its conclusion.

Whenever you are confronted by a passage where you think there is an argument from analogy, then, you should first standardize it: set out its premises and its conclusion. Once that is done, you will know that the primary subject is the item in the analogy that is also the subject of the conclusion, while the analogue is the thing with which it is being compared. The predicate of the conclusion is the targetted predicate, and has to be kept separate from the similarities that are explicitly mentioned in the first premise or analogy.

This argument pattern does not have any neat rules for assessment. Because the crucial connection between the primary subject and the analogue is not simple predication but an analogy, we cannot decide, simply on the basis of form, whether the argument is valid or not. In fact, no argument from analogy is ever deductive. The premise can never *require* the conclusion.

Recall that an analogy mentions similarities between things that are otherwise quite different. Because it compares things that are both alike and unlike, we cannot know simply from the structure of the argument whether the targetted predicate will be one of the ways the two things are alike, or whether in this case they are unlike.

Thus the argument *form* can provide no answer to the question: do the premises validly establish the conclusion? They may be quite misleading, because an important difference is veiled; or they may be useful in trying to reach new insights, because the similarity is significant. To assess whether the premises provide good grounds for the conclusion we must look closely in each case at the *actual analogy used*.

In the *Dialogues Concerning Natural Religion,* David Hume had another of his characters, Philo, submit Cleanthes's argument to critical examination. This involved two different strategies.

In the first place, Philo pointed out that there were many ways in which the universe was not like a machine. There are times when things do not work well: there are false starts, as when animals give birth to defective young; there are events of positive destruction, like hurricanes, volcanoes, and floods; there are occasions when natural forces, each with its own internal structure, come in conflict, so that one or both are frustrated, as when a flock of sheep eats all the available grass early in an unusually dry summer. This suggests either that the universe is not well planned, placing the reference to a thoughtful designer in question; or that the designer is not so very attractive after all, hardly like the God that Cleanthes claims to worship.

The second kind of criticism Philo advances went beyond simply pointing out the differences between the primary subject and the analogue. He suggested that quite different analogies are possible: "The world plainly resembles more an animal or vegetable, than it does a watch or a knitting-loom. Its cause, therefore, it is more probable, resembles the cause of the former." This leads to a quite different argument and conclusion: "The cause of the former [the animal or vegetable] is generation or vegetation. The cause, therefore, of the world we may infer to be some thing similar or analogous to generation or vegetation."

An analogy focuses on one set of relations within the primary subject and looks for a similar pattern elsewhere. But if the primary subject is complex and diverse, like the universe, there are many patterns and relations that could be highlighted through an analogy. The task then is to decide which is more significant and important, which represents more closely what the primary subject (in this case, the world) really is.

After reading Hume's *Dialogues* it is tempting to think that all arguments from analogy are quite weak. In every case one can point to differences that call the inference into question. But we should be cautious about drawing that conclusion. For, in fact, many arguments from analogy do lead us along pathways that are ultimately correct. For example, when Galileo was looking at some stars that moved in peculiar ways around Jupiter, he was quite puzzled, until he finally drew an analogy between the way these "stars" move around Jupiter and the way the planets move around the sun, and the moon moves around the earth. Using this analogy he made correct predictions about their future locations. Since those predictions were based on the assumption that the "stars" were really Jupiter's moons, they were derived by way of an argument from analogy.

Because arguments from analogy can be strong as well as weak, we need to spend some time thinking about how we should assess them. How can we decide whether an argument of this sort provides good grounds for its conclusion or not?

We start by recalling that an analogy compares two different things. It states a similarity, but implies a difference. The similarity and difference both now become important.

The first premise states similarities that we already know about. After all, an argument will not be very effective if its premises are not true, or look questionable. It will be plausible only if we have good reason for believing the premises to be true. Since the analogy is the first premise in an argument from analogy, the reasoning would not be very convincing if it used an analogy that was patently absurd: that two things were said to be similar in ways that our experience had shown to be quite different. It is to the advantage of the person presenting the argument to spell out those similarities that are most obvious, and with which people would easily agree.

Since the second premise also needs to be acceptable, the analogue should be known to have the targetted predicate.

Once we have two acceptable premises we must decide whether they provide good grounds for the conclusion. The critical question concerns the relation between the targetted predicate and the similarities mentioned or assumed in the first premise.

Recall that a second feature of an analogy is that it shows how various things are related. In an argument from analogy, that relationship is extended. The similarities include not only those mentioned in the first premise. They are supposed to extend to the targetted predicate as well. However, if the targetted predicate is one of the ways the analogue is *different from* the primary subject, then the argument is misleading. So the question to ask is whether, in the analogue, that targetted predicate is closely related or not to the similarities mentioned in the original analogy. The more closely they are connected, the more likely will be the conclusion.

To assess the argument, then, we must consider carefully the way the targetted predicate fits into the analogue. Is it more closely connected with the similarities mentioned in the first premise? In that case the argument is fairly strong. Is it related more closely to those aspects of the analogue in which it is different from the primary subject? In that case the argument is weak. We need not only take into account the similarities mentioned and assumed in the analogy. We must also think carefully and critically to identify important differences which are ignored in the first premise.

To illustrate let us consider several inferences from analogy.

We can feel our own pain or doubt or anger, but not that of others. For we observe only the way their bodies behave, not how their minds work. Yet others behave as if they experience doubt, anger, pain and other states of mind. Their behaviour is similar to the way we express our own mental states. We may reasonably attribute these bodily expressions, in others as in ourselves, to states of consciousness. Thus we may infer that other people have minds and mental experiences similar to our own.

We can structure the argument this way:

P1: Other people are like us in that their behaviour is similar to ours.
P2: Our behaviour is an expression of our feelings and emotions.
C: So we conclude that other people also have feelings and emotions that are expressed in their behaviour.

In this argument, the targetted predicate is "having feelings and emotions". The similarities mentioned in the analogy are particular forms of "behaviour". The passage, however, goes further. The second premise points out that we consistently find that our behaviour is closely connected with particular pains and pleasures. The similarities and the targetted predicate are intimately connected in our experience (which, of course, is the analogue). Because the connection is strong in the case of the analogue, "ourselves", it is likely that the targetted predicate will also apply to the primary subject, "other people".

On the other hand, we might not be so comfortable with a different argument from analogy:

P1: Calculators are like us in that they can add, subtract, multiply and divide.
P2: We can write poetry.
C: So calculators can write poetry.

Here a few minutes' thought suggests that our ability to write poetry is more closely related to our imagination, our feelings, and our ability to sympathize with other people than to our ability to do arithmetical operations. And calculators are different from us in that they do not have imagination, feelings, or sympathy. In other words, the targetted predicate is more closely related to the differences between analogue and primary subject, than to the similarities mentioned in the analogy. So we assess the argument as weak because the premises do not provide good support for the conclusion.

To sum up, then, an argument from analogy has a definite formal structure. The first premise states an analogy; the second premise predicates another feature of one of the things being compared, or analogue. That feature is then predicated of the other thing, or primary subject.

To decide whether an argument from analogy provides good grounds for its conclusion, we must consider the relation between the targetted predicate and the similarities mentioned in the analogy. Are these closely connected in the analogue? Or is the targetted predicate more tied up with the way the analogue differs from the primary subject?

At times, it will be easy to answer that question one way or another. At other times, however, it will be more difficult, and we may have to explore further before we can decide. Knowing that the relationship is not clear is itself an achievement, though. By being cautious, we can ensure that we are not beguiled by attractive comparisons.

Being cautious requires that we carefully follow a number of steps:

1. Standardize the argument: identify the conclusion; then put the analogy in the first premise along with the similarities expressly stated and those clearly assumed; finally enter the second premise by combining the analogue from the first premise with the targetted predicate from the conclusion. (Frequently we have to reconstruct the second premise from the rest of the argument.)

2. Identify as carefully as possible the ways in which the analogue is different from the primary subject.

3. Consider the targetted predicate together with the similarities from the first premise and the differences you have just identified and decide which it is closer to, and how strong the connection of closeness is. The closer it is to the similarities, the stronger the argument; the closer to the differences, the weaker it is.

There will be no clear cut answer. You have to decide based on the evidence you have before you, and that requires an act of judgement. You should be able, however, to defend your judgement if you are challenged.

EXERCISE:

In each of the following passages, set out the argument from analogy in standard form, indicating clearly what are the primary subject, the analogue, the similarities and the targetted predicate. Then assess the argument to decide whether it provides good grounds for the conclusion or not. Give reasons for your assessment.

EXAMPLE: "Would it not be most unnatural, if a fire were to break out in a city, and everyone were to keep still and let it burn on and on, whatever might be burnt, simply because they had not the mayor's authority, or because the fire, perchance broke out in the mayor's house? Is not every citizen bound in this case to rouse and call in the rest? How much more should this be done in the spiritual city of Christ, if a fire of offence breaks out, either at the Pope's government or wherever it may! The like happens if an enemy attacks a town. The first to rouse up the rest earns glory and thanks. Why then should not he earn glory that descries the coming of our enemies from hell and rouses and summons all Christians?" M. Luther, *Address to the Christian Nobility of the Germanic Nation*, "The Third Wall". [Assume that the rhetorical questions are equivalent statements.]

Standard Form:

Premise 1: The church (PS) is like a city (A) in that it involves a number of people organised as a community with a government (S). (The similarities have been assumed and not expressly stated.)

Premise 2: In a city (A), when a fire breaks out or an enemy attacks, every citizen has a responsibility to call people together to fight it without waiting for the government (TP).

Conclusion: Therefore in the church (PS) every member has the responsibility to lead the charge against attacks on the church without waiting for the initiative of the Pope (TP).

Assessment: The church is like a city in being an organized community of people. However, it has another purpose as well. It is not simply responsible for the economic and social life of people, but for their spiritual well-being. In addition it is not geographically located in one area, but extends over many towns and many countries. Further, the spiritual attacks on the church are not as clear-cut and obvious as a fire or an enemy attack. These differences suggest that the analogy is not strong, for the targetted predicate is more closely connected with geographical compactness and economic and social well-being than with simply being an organized community. (Other assessments are also possible, depending on the kind of analysis followed.)

1. Industry is like a garden in that it has periods of prosperity and periods of drought. In the same way that a garden needs careful cultivation to thrive, industry requires government regulation and the development of good programs for research, transportation and communication.

2. Mental skills are like physical skills in that they are based on innate aptitudes and can be developed by training. We do not think that everyone should have an equal right to play for the varsity hockey team. So we should not expect that everyone has an equal right to attend university.

3. Being virtuous is like navigating a ship. One needs to develop good judgement through experience. But you cannot learn to navigate a ship by studying theory in a classroom. Therefore there is no point in providing moral education in the schools.

4. "Religion would thus be the universal obsessional neurosis of humanity; like the obsessional neurosis of children, it arose out of the Oedipus complex, out of the relation to the father. If this view is right, it is to be supposed that a turning away from religion is bound to occur with the fatal inevitability of a process of growth, and that we find ourselves at this very juncture in the middle of that phase of development." S. Freud, *The Future of an Illusion*.

5. "Mencius said to King Hsüan of Ch'i, 'Supposing one of your ministers had gone on a journey to Ch'u, leaving his wife and children with a friend, and upon returning found his family starving, what do you think he should do?' The King said,'He should cut off all relations with that friend.' Mencius said, 'Suppose now that the Leader of the Knights had no control over the knights, then what would you do?'

The King said, 'I should dismiss him.' Mencius said, 'Suppose now the kingdom to be ill-governed, what then should be done?' The King turned to his courtiers and spoke of other things." *Mencius*, tr. W.A.C.H. Dobson.

6. In the 1980's strenuous efforts are being made to preserve and renovate historic buildings in Canada and other countries. Influential groups are successfully lobbying to preserve species of plants and animals which face extinction. We therefore believe it to be eminently reasonable that similar efforts be made to support and reinvigorate threatened languages and cultures. The very diversity of the human race — while it may sometimes complicate life — is just as worthy of support as is the diversity of plant and animal life.

7. "However great may be the force of external pressures on people, we still need to understand the way in which those people respond to the pressures. Infection can bring on fever, but only in creatures with a suitable circulatory system. Like fever, [so] spite, resentment, envy, avarice, cruelty, meanness, hatred and the rest are themselves complex states, and they produce complex activities. Outside events may indeed bring them on, but, like other malfunctions, they would not develop if we were not prone to them." Mary Midgley, *Wickedness*. Reprinted with permission, Routledge.

8. "It is the maxim of every prudent master of a family, never to attempt to make at home what it will cost him more to make than to buy. The taylor does not attempt to make his own shoes, but buys them from the shoemaker. The shoemaker does not attempt to make his own clothes, but employs a taylor. The farmer attempts to make neither the one nor the other, but employs those different ar-

tificers. All of them find it for their interest to employ their whole industry in a way in which they have some advantage over their neighbours, and to purchase with a part of its produce, or what is the same thing, with the price of a part of it, whatever else they have occasion for.

"What is prudence in the conduct of every private family, can scarce be folly in that of a great kingdom. If a foreign country can supply us with a commodity cheaper than we ourselves can make it, better buy it of them with some part of the produce of our own industry, employed in a way in which we have some advantage." A. Smith, *The Wealth of Nations*.

9. "We have an inheritable crown, an inheritable peerage, and a House of Commons and a people inheriting privileges, franchises and liberties from a long line of ancestors.... Our political system is placed in a just correspondence and symmetry with the order of the world and with the mode of existence decreed to a permanent body composed of transitory parts, wherein, by the disposition of a stupendous wisdom, moulding together the great mysterious incorporation of the human race, the whole, at one time, is never old or middle-aged or young, but, in a condition of unchangeable constancy, moves on through the varied tenor of perpetual decay, fall, renovation, and progression. Thus, by preserving the method of nature in the conduct of the state, in what we improve we are never wholly new; in what we retain we are never wholly obsolete. By adhering in this manner and on those principles to our forefathers, we are guided not by the superstition of antiquarians, but by the spirit of philosophic analogy. In this choice of inheritance we have given to our frame of polity the image of a relation in blood, binding up the constitution of our country with our dearest domestic ties, adopting out fundamental laws into the bosom of our family affections,

keeping inseparable and cherishing with the warmth of all their combined and mutually reflected charities our state, our hearths, our sepulchres, and our altars." E. Burke, *Reflections on the Revolution in France*.

10. "All the members of whole classes are connected together by a chain of affinities, and all can be classed on the same principle, in groups subordinate to groups. Throughout whole classes various structures are formed on the same pattern, and at a very early age the embryos closely resemble each other. Therefore I cannot doubt that the theory of descent with modification embraces all the members of the same great class or kingdom. I believe that animals are descended from at most only four or five progenitors, and plants from an equal or lesser number.

"Analogy would lead me one step farther, namely, to the belief that all animals and plants are descended from some one prototype. But analogy may be a deceitful guide. Nevertheless all living things have much in common, in their chemical composition, their cellular structure, their laws of growth, and their liability to injurious influences. With all organic beings, excepting perhaps some of the very lowest, sexual reproduction seems to be essentially similar. If we look even to the two main divisions — namely, to the animal and vegetable kingdoms — certain low forms are so far intermediate in character that naturalists have disputed to which kingdom they should be referred. Therefore on the principle of natural selection with divergence of character, it does not seem incredible that, from some such low and intermediate form, both animals and plants may have been developed; and, if we admit this, we must likewise admit that all the organic beings which have ever lived on this earth may be descended from some one primordial form. But this inference is chiefly grounded on analogy, and it is immaterial whether or not it be accepted."

C. Darwin, *The Origin of the Species*. [adapted]

11. "If man can, with almost complete assurance, predict phenomena when he knows their laws, and if, even when he does not, he can still, with great expectation of success, forecast the future on the basis of his experience of the past, why, then, should it be regarded as a fantastic undertaking to sketch, with some pretense to truth, the future destiny of man on the basis of his history? The sole foundation for belief in the natural sciences is this idea, that the general laws directing the phenomena of the universe, known or unknown, are necessary and constant. Why should this principle be any less true for the development of the intellectual and moral faculties of man than for other operations of nature? Since beliefs founded on past experience of like conditions provide the only rule of conduct for the wisest of men, why should the philosopher be forbidden to base his conjectures on these same foundations, so long as he does not attribute to them a certainty superior to that warranted by the number, the constancy, and the accuracy of his observations?" A.N. de Condorcet, *The Progress of the Human Mind*. (Convert the rhetorical questions into their appropriate answers.)

CHAPTER 3

REPLIES TO OBJECTIONS

Quite often we criticize someone else's argument from analogy by pointing out how the targetted predicate is connected with the differences between analogue and primary subject rather than with their similarities. This is what Thomas Hobbes was doing in the passage below.

He imagined that his opponent had presented an argument of this sort: Bees and ants are like humans in that they are social creatures. Bees and ants survive without a government. So humans do not need a government either.

Hobbes replied by showing that the differences between bees and ants on the one hand and humans on the other are more important than the similarities:

"To which I answer: First that men are continually in competition for honour and dignities, which these creatures are not; and consequently among men there arises on the ground envy and hatred and finally war, but among these [bees and ants] not so.

"Secondly, that among these creatures the common good differs not from the private; and being by nature inclined to their private, they procure thereby the common benefit. But man, whose joy consists in comparing himself with other men, can relish nothing but what is eminent.

"Thirdly, that these creatures, having not, as man, the use of reason, do not see nor think they see any fault in the administration of their common business; whereas among men, there are very many that think themselves wiser and abler to govern the public better than the rest."

Hobbes here argues that the differences that separate humans from bees and ants have more to do with the kind of government they require, than the simple fact that they are living social creatures. Humans crave honour and are prone to envy; they distinguish their own fortune from that of society; and through reasoning they think themselves better than their neighbours. The social animals share none of these characteristics.

Thus Hobbes refuted an argument from analogy by showing that the targetted predicate was more closely connected with the differences between primary subject and analogue than with their similarities.

The same technique is used in response to other challenges as well.

An opponent suggests that your position has unfortunate or false implications. Using the logical form of *modus tollens*, or denying the consequent, he or she then concludes that your position is to be rejected:

Premise 1: If your position A is true, then B would be the case.
Premise 2: But B is false (or highly improbable).
Conclusion: So position A is unacceptable.

In reply you show that the objection does not in fact apply to the point you are making, because your opponent has missed an important difference that distinguishes your position from the one (A) being attacked in the first premise. The two positions are only analogous, not identical; and the differences implicit in the analogy are significant.

St. Thomas Aquinas was an expert at drawing such distinctions. In his *Summa Theologica* he started out every section by listing objections to the position he would eventually espouse. Then, at the end, he replied to those objections. In almost every case he did so by distinguishing his thesis from the one being attacked. He did not challenge the reasoning of his opponent. He simply said that it did not apply.

For example, when discussing the question: *Whether it is a sin to take interest [he uses the word "usury"] for money lent?* he cited the following objection:

> Silver made into coins does not differ in kind from silver made into a vessel. But it is lawful to accept a price for the loan of a silver vessel. Therefore it is also lawful to accept a price for the loan of a silver coin. Therefore usury is not in itself a sin.

Aquinas did not move directly to a reply. He first drew his own general conclusion: "To take interest for money lent is unjust because this is to sell what does not exist, and this evidently leads to inequality which is contrary to justice." Having established this point he then came to the objection, and he made his reply in these words:

> The principal use of a silver vessel is not its consumption, and so one may lawfully sell its use while retaining one's ownership of it. On the other hand the principal use of silver money is sinking it in exchange, so that it is not lawful to sell its use and at the same time expect the restitution of the amount lent. It must be observed, however, that the secondary use of silver vessels may be an exchange,

and such use may not lawfully be sold. In like manner there may be some secondary use of silver money; for instance, a man might lend coins for show, or to be used as security.

The objection stated that silver made into coins was no different from silver made into bowls and goblets. But St. Thomas drew a distinction between renting out something that has an independent use and can be returned, and lending money, whose sole purpose is to be spent and used in trade. In the first case the original owner retains his ownership; in the second case he transfers ownership and the right of use. And while he may justly expect to have the same amount of money returned, he cannot charge extra for its use, because that would be charging twice for the same thing.

In our modern capitalistic world that distinction between something where use is consumption and something where use is simply enjoyment seems trivial, and we have had no problem with accepting usury, or charging interest on money lent. But for St. Thomas it made a considerable difference, and his reply to the objection was built on that distinction.

The objection started from a similarity. It noticed that one could charge rent for the use of a silver bowl or a silver bracelet and assumed that, all silver being the same, one could charge as well for the use of silver money. Aquinas agreed that one can legitimately charge rent for the use of a bowl or bracelet. But by showing that consumption and enjoyment have quite distinct moral characteristics, he claimed that the objection did not apply in this case.

He argued that the fact that silver was involved does not make the two cases essentially the same. The objector had assumed some general principle about the use of silver; bracelets and coins are two instances of that principle. In reply Thomas said that the objector had appealed to an analogy, not to a universal rule. And the argument from analogy was ineffective because in this case the difference is more significant than the similarity.

This is a common pattern when people reply to objections. We can represent it this way:

Premise 1: The objector has assumed that because PS is the same as A it shares the targetted predicate TP.
Premise 2: PS and A are not identical but analogues, different though similar.
Premise 3: The difference between PS and A is more closely connected to TP than the similarity is.
Conclusion: Therefore TP does not apply to PS.

In our case:

Premise 1: The objection states that coins and vessels, being silver, can both be lent for a charge.
Premise 2: While the coins and vessels are both silver, when vessels are lent for use they can be returned, but when coins are lent they will be given away in exchange and cannot therefore be returned after use.
Premise 3: It is more appropriate to charge rent for temporary use than for something given permanently (which needs only to be replaced).
Conclusion: Therefore interest, or charge for use, does not apply to the lending of money.

To assess a reply to an objection of this sort we concentrate on the third premise. We apply once again our procedure for assessing arguments from analogy. Are the similarities or the differences more closely connected with the targetted predicate?

As we have already suggested, our contemporary capitalistic world finds it difficult to appreciate the distinction between consumption and enjoyment that St. Thomas made so much of. The distinction is there, to be sure, but it does not seem to be significant in the case where we are talking about charging rent for use. In this way we challenge the third premise. A silver bowl and a silver coin may be analogous and not instances of a single principle, but in this argument, their similarities are more significant than their differences, and have a greater bearing on whether we should charge interest for their use.

In other words, where, as here a reply to an objection argues that there is an analogy rather than a simple identity, we can use the rules for assessing arguments from analogy to evaluate its claim.

Objections to a position generally involve a modus tollens. *First one draws some implications from that position; then one shows that at least one of those implications is false or unreliable. Together these two steps are used to refute the original theory.*

In replying to an objection, one may challenge its assumption that the position with the false implications is the same as the position in question. The reply claims that they are not the same but a covert analogy. The things that have been identified are also to be distinguished. And these differences are significant for the point in question.

When assessing such a reply to an objection, we follow the procedure used in arguments from analogy. Is the difference closely connected to the implication drawn, or are the similarities more important? Are the differences so trivial that the similarity really becomes a full fledged identity, or are they recognizable and in need of being acknowledged in an analogy?

EXERCISE:

In the following replies to objections identify the similarity or identity assumed by the objection, the targetted predicate, and the difference that is to transform it into an analogy. Assess the argument to determine whether the difference does justify rejecting the objection.

EXAMPLE: "It might be objected that everything produced is subject to destruction, as has been shown; consequently the Universe, having had a beginning, must come to an end. This axiom cannot be applied according to our views. We do not hold that the Universe came into existence, like all things in Nature, as the result of laws of Nature. For whatever owes its existence to the action of physical laws is, according to the same laws, subject to destruction: the same law which caused the existence of a thing after a period of non-existence, is also the cause that the thing is not permanent; since the previous non-existence proves that the nature of that thing does not necessitate its permanent existence. According to our theory, taught in Scripture, the existence or non-existence of things depends solely on the will of God and not on fixed laws, and, therefore, it does not follow that God must destroy the Universe after having created it from nothing. It depends on His will. He may, according to His desire, or according to the decree of His wisdom, either destroy it, or allow it to exist, and it is therefore possible that He will preserve the Universe forever, and let it exist permanently as He Himself exists." Moses Maimonides, *The Guide for the Perplexed*.

Structure:

Similarity: The Universe is like everything produced in that it has a beginning.
Targetted Predicate: Both must come to an end.
Difference: The Universe did not come into existence naturally, in the way things produced came to be, but simply because God willed it.

Assessment: The Universe includes the laws of nature that govern the way other things come to be. Therefore what happens to it as a whole is different from what happens to the various things in the universe. There is, then, no need to conclude that the Universe will come to an end. The difference between the Universe and things produced is significant enough to reject the objection. (That difference may mean that the Universe has no beginning either.)

1. You say that because most cars require an engine job after 200,000 kilometres mine will as well. But my car has a diesel engine, and diesel engines have fewer moving parts than gasoline engines do. Therefore I should be able to drive my car for a while longer before major repairs are necessary.

2. The opposition party say that there is nothing wrong with a budget deficit, since it is like the mortgage that we arrange when we buy a house. They claim that we simply repay the loan while we are using the building. But we only need to incur a mortgage once in our lives, and we progressively reduce our household debt as we use our income to pay it off. The government, however, lasts over many

lifetimes. When it keeps incurring a deficit every year, it never has any surplus to retire old debts.

3. The bus companies claim that there should be no subsidy for passenger trains but that they should be forced to compete on the open market, and go under if they cannot break even. However, the trains have to build and maintain their own roadbed, while the buses use public highways. Therefore their objection does not hold, and subsidies are in order.

4. *Objection*: Anyone may lawfully accept a thing which its owner freely gives him. Now he who accepts the loan, freely gives the interest. Therefore he who lends may lawfully take the interest.

   Reply: He who pays interest does not pay it voluntarily, but under a certain necessity, in so far as he needs to borrow money which the owner is unwilling to lend without interest. St. Thomas Aquinas, *Summa Theologica* [adapted].

5. *Objection*: "Sartre declares that every man is free, that there is no way of his not being free. When he wants to escape his destiny, he is still freely fleeing it. Does not this presence of a so to speak natural freedom contradict the notion of ethical freedom? What meaning can there be in the words *to will oneself* free, since at the beginning we *are* free? It is contradictory to set freedom up as something conquered if at first it is something given.

   Reply: This objection would mean something only if freedom were a thing or a quality naturally attached to a thing. Then, in effect, one would either have it or not have it. But the fact is that it merges with the very movement of this ambiguous reality which is called existence and which *is* only by making itself be; to such an extent that it is precisely only by having to be conquered that it gives itself. To will oneself free is to effect the transition from nature to morality by establishing a genuine freedom on the original upsurge of our existence." Simone de Beauvoir, *The Ethics of Ambiguity*.

6. "If an individual, says Grotius, can alienate his liberty and become the slave of a master, why should not a whole people be able to alienate theirs, and become subject to a king? In this there are many equivocal terms requiring explanation; but let us confine ourselves to the word *alienate*. To alienate is to give or sell. Now, a man who becomes another's slave does not give himself; he sells himself at the very least for his subsistence. But why does a nation sell itself? So far from a king supplying his subjects with their subsistence, he draws his from them; and, according to Rabelais, a king does not live on a little. Do subjects, then, give up their persons on condition that their property also shall be taken? I do not see what is left for them to keep." J.-J. Rousseau, *The Social Contract*.

7. John Stuart Mill, in his work *On Liberty*, argues against the censorship of ideas. He then outlines in some detail a possible objection to his thesis which ends this way:

> "There is no such thing as absolute certainty, but there is assurance sufficient for the purposes of human life. We may, and must, assume our opinions to be true for the guidance of our own conduct: and it is assuming no more when we forbid men to pervert society by the propagation of opinions which we regard as false and pernicious."

To this objection, Mill made his reply:

"I answer, that it is assuming very much more. There is the greatest difference between presuming an opinion to be true, because, with every opportunity for contesting it, it has not been refuted, and assuming its truth for the purpose of not permitting its refutation. Complete liberty of contradicting and disproving our opinion is the very condition which justifies us in assuming its truth for purposes of action; and on no other terms can a being with human faculties have any rational assurance of being right."

8. "Before we proceed with the systematic comparison of our twenty-one societies, which is the purpose of this book, we must meet certain possible objections. The first and simplest argument against the procedure we propose may be stated thus: 'These societies have no common characteristic beyond the fact that all of them are "intelligible fields of study", and this characteristic is so vague and general that it can be turned to no practical account.'

"The answer is that societies which are 'intelligible fields of study' are a genus within which our twenty-one representatives constitute one particular species. Societies of this species are commonly called civilizations, to distinguish them from primitive societies which are also 'intelligible fields of study' and which form another, in fact *the* other, species within this genus. Our twenty-one societies must, therefore, have one specific feature in common that they alone are in process of civilization.

"Another difference between the two species at once suggests itself. The number of known civilizations is small. The number of known primitive societies is vastly greater. In 1915 three Western anthropologists, setting out to make a comparative study of primitive societies and confining themselves to those about which adequate information was available, registered about 650, most of them alive today. It is impossible to form any conception of the number of primitive societies which must have come into and passed out of existence since man first became human, perhaps 300,000 years ago, but it is evident that the numerical preponderance of primitive societies over civilizations is overwhelming.

"Almost equally overwhelming is the preponderance of civilizations over primitive societies in their individual dimensions. The primitive societies, in their legions, are relatively short-lived, are restricted to relatively narrow geographical areas and embrace relatively small numbers of human beings. It is probable that if we could take a census of the membership of the five living civilizations up to date, during the small number of centuries through which they have yet lived, we should find that each of our Leviathans, singly, has embraced more human beings than could be mustered by all the primitive societies taken together since the emergence of the human race. However, we are studying not individuals but societies, and the significant fact for our purpose is that the number of societies in process of civilization known to have existed has been comparatively small." A. Toynbee, *A Study of History*, Abridgement by D.C. Somervell.

9. "Now the most absurd argument, replied Cleanthes, in the hands of a man of ingenuity and invention, may acquire an air of probability! Are you not aware, Philo, that it became necessary for Copernicus and his first disciples to prove the similarity of the terrestrial and celestial matter; because several philosophers, blinded by old systems, and supported by some sensible appearances, had denied this similarity? But [are you not also aware] that it is by no means necessary, that theists should prove the similarity of the works of nature to those of art; because this similarity

is self-evident and undeniable? The same matter, a like form: What more is requisite to show an analogy between their causes, and to ascertain the origin of all things from a divine purpose and intention?" D. Hume, *Dialogues concerning Natural Religion.*

CHAPTER 4

INDUCTION

For the past five years, in the early spring, an eccentric tulip has bloomed in a corner of my back lawn. Now I have come to expect it. As the weather warms up through April and into May I look for the telltale leaves, the developing bud, and finally the bright red flower.

My expectation is the result of reasoning. And the kind of reasoning involved has its own peculiar name: induction. From a number of past experiences I infer something that is not yet experienced.

In this case, I infer one new instance: that the tulip will bloom this coming spring. But I might extend the inference further: I could say that the tulip will bloom *every* spring.

While we might not be quite so bold as to make the inference for every single spring with regard to my tulip, we do so with lots of other things. Since every cow we have ever seen chews its cud, we confidently assume that all cows chew their cud. That, too, is an induction.

Inductions are of various sorts. The kind we have mentioned here we call simple inductions. In them we extend features we have noticed in our previous experience to cases unseen. We *generalize*.

The pattern of inductive reasoning is not unfamiliar. It is simply one form of argument from analogy.

Premise 1: This spring is like the past five springs in that the days are getting longer, the weather is getting warmer, and there is a lot of gentle rain.
Premise 2: In the past five springs a red tulip has blossomed in my back lawn.
Conclusion: So this spring the tulip will bloom.

Or:

Premise 1: All cattle are like the cows I have seen in basic physical features.
Premise 2: Cows I have seen chew their cud.
Conclusion: So all cattle chew their cud.

There is a shift in pattern, however, from the analogical arguments which we considered before. In a simple induction there are fewer differences between primary subject and analogue, and more similarities. Indeed, there are so many similarities that we talk of *categories* of things, such as "spring" or "cow". Since the category identifies the primary subject with the analogue we hardly need to specify their similarities. For those similarities are contained in the definition of the category.

The differences in a simple induction are now thought of as different instances of the category. The analogue refers to those instances — the springs or cows — we have already encountered, those about which we have some knowledge. The primary subject points to one or more cases we know nothing about, because they lie either in the future or outside the range of our experience. In an induction we call those examples of the category in the analogue the *sample*, and those identified by the primary subject the *population* of the induction. The population can be a single instance or several, as in my prediction about the coming spring. Or it can be all instances of the category: all cows. With this shift in terminology, the pattern of argument in simple induction becomes:

Premise 1: The sample is of the same category as the population.
Premise 2: The sample has a targetted predicate.
Conclusion: So the population has the targetted predicate.

The first premise is seldom, if ever, expressly stated. It is usually simply assumed that a sample is similar to the population. One spring is like all springs; one cow like all cows. Nonetheless, in standardizing it is useful to make that premise explicit. By spelling out the similarities between the population and the sample we have a basis for assessing the inference. Therefore, the first step in any standardizing is to identify the category into which both the sample and the population fall. Where the inference is a full generalization, the category is usually mentioned in the noun or noun phrase that follows the adjective "each," "every," or "all" (such as "cows").

Simple inductions, then, work with categories; and the analogue is simply a sample of the category. This may suggest that the differences in an argument from analogy have been dissolved into outright similarity, or identity. Nonetheless, important differences may well emerge. Almost all discussions of simple induction recall an episode in western cultural history. Until the eighteenth century, Europeans confidently assumed by induction that all swans were white, because all the swans native to Europe were white. When they arrived in Australia, however, they discovered swans which were black. The inductive conclusion proved to be wrong. Some of the population ("all swans") were considerably different in colour from the sample.

We have distinguished sample from population as those things which we *do* know about from our experience, and those we have not yet encountered. And we make an induction whenever we expect that things or events in the future will resemble things or events in our past. Our reasoning is confirmed, then, when our anticipations are satisfied—when the only important difference is between known and unknown. It is misleading whenever we are surprised by unexpected results—when other significant dissimilarities emerge.

Inductions fail for two reasons. In the example of the swans we found a situation where the targetted predicate was not a defining feature of the category. It was more closely connected to variable characteristics than to those that identify the species.

But other times we discover that the population is not of the same category as the sample. We pick up what looks like an apple and start to eat it, only to find that it is acid and bitter. Instead of an apple, we have bitten into a quince. We had falsely *categorized* or *classified* the new instance. For we connected it with the sample of apples in our experience, only to find that the population in our inference has come from a different category altogether and so our reasoning was wrong.

Indeed, quite often it is when inductions fail that we discover new categories to be necessary. This is the reasoning biologists and anthropologists use when they identify new species. A distinctive leaf, or a peculiar form of reproduction will differentiate one kind of iris from another.

This practice of creating new categories (or classification, as it is called) happens in more informal ways as well. When, on October 19, 1987, the stock market dropped 500 points, many people drew an immediate induction that the crash of 1929 would be repeated; and investors scurried for shelter. But as time wore on, analysts noted that there were quite different features this time around, and they talked about a "melt down" rather than a "crash". A new category had been created.

This, then, helps us to clarify the kind of assessment we can make of an induction. Since simple inductions may fail either because the targetted predicate is not an invariable feature of the category, or because sample and population are not of the same category, we should ask two questions: Are sample and population of the same category? (Is this fruit really an apple, or is it something different?) And: How closely connected is the targetted predicate to the identifying characteristics of the category? (Is colour an essential characteristic of a genus of birds such as swans?) Simply on the basis of what we already know about the sample and the population, we can then have some idea how successful the induction will be—we can be more confident in making predictions about the future.

In answering those questions we are just applying our method of assessment for arguments from analogy. The similarities between the primary subject and the analogue have been collected together into the category. The differences are reduced to a matter of individual variations.

The first question asks, then, whether we should really classify the sample and the population in the same category. In the process of spelling out the first premise, do we have a category that is sufficiently well defined that we can easily recognise which things belong to it? Or is the category so vague and ill-defined that differences may well be more important than the apparent similarity. There are so many kinds of rounded, firm fruit gathered from trees that it is dangerous to assume that all will be alike. Economic ups and downs vary so much, depending on the specific historical circumstances, that it is difficult to identify features which would categorize them effectively.

The second question asks whether the targetted predicate is likely to be another defining characteristic of the category, or whether it is something that could be an individual variable. In the case of the swans, for example, colour may be used to identify some categories or species, but not all. Therefore the colour white is not necessarily one of the features that characterize swans.

The two questions are related. For categories can be quite general and all-inclusive, or they can be quite specific. And we can respond to unsuccessful inductions either by making the category more general, or by making it more specific. Western Europeans generalized further their classification of swans. But ornithologists may restrict their earlier category of sparrows, and create a new one, when they discover one that does not have the expected black stripes on its wings. In other words, when we find some feature in a population that does not directly match the sample with which we started, we may either consider the targetted predicate inessential or adjust our categories.

This way of shifting from one way of handling the evidence to another can be illustrated from anthropology. Anthropologists at first classified *Australopithecus* as an aberrant ape rather than a hominid (or incipient human) because of its small brain volume, and a pelvic bone that did not seem appropriate to an upright posture. It was placed in a separate category. Subsequently, however, it was realized that small brain size did not remove a species from the class of hominids, for our human ancestors must have had smaller brains at some stage. As well the differences between the pelvis of the *Australopithecus* and the human pelvis did not mean that this species were not bipeds. Further evidence suggested that they regularly walked upright. So the differences that initially required separate categories became secondary, and so members of this particular species were reclassified as incipient humans.

In a simple induction we move from a sample to a population. The sample is like the population in being of the same kind or category. Once we identify a predicate in the sample, we then extend that predicate to the population, whether that is a single thing (my tulip next spring), or the category as a whole (cows or swans).

We can assess a simple induction by considering how closely related the targetted predicate is to the defining characteristics of the category; and by considering whether the population is in fact of the same kind or category as the sample.

A more critical test is to take a further sample from the population to see whether the targetted predicate is found there as well. If this does not support the induction, it may mean that the sample and population are not of the same category or kind, or that the targetted predicate is not characteristic of the category.

EXERCISE:

For the following simple inductions, standardize the argument, and indicate clearly the sample, the population, the category, and the targetted predicate. Then assess the argument by asking two questions: Is the category well enough defined to make an induction possible? Is the targetted predicate closely connected with the defining features of the category?

EXAMPLE: "Neither is it to be forgotten that in every age natural philosophy has had a troublesome and hard to deal with adversary namely, superstition, and the blind and immoderate zeal of religion. For we see among the Greeks that those who first proposed to men's then uninitiated ears the natural causes for thunder and for storms were thereupon found guilty of impiety. Nor was much more forebearance shown by some of the ancient fathers of the Christian church to those who on most convincing grounds maintained that the earth was round." F. Bacon, *The New Organon.*

Standardize:

1st Premise: The ancient Greeks (S^1) and the early Church (S^2) are two examples of every age (P). ["Age" is the category.]

2nd Premise: The Greeks (S^1) called those who gave natural explanations of thunder storms impious (TP^1); and the early Christian fathers (S^2) attacked those who said the earth was round (TP^2).

Conclusion: So in every age (P) those who investigate natural phenomena and causes have a difficult time with religious superstition (TP).

Assessment: It is very difficult to know what exactly is meant by an "age". Since the category is not clearly defined the induction is not strong.

While there may well be a tendency for those who accept traditional beliefs to make life difficult for those who investigate things scientifically, the feature of religion condemning natural science is not closely connected with anything that might define an age. In other words the conclusion has not been established by the induction but relies instead on unexpressed assumptions.

1. On the evening of President Reagan's election in 1980, a person interviewed on television made the following

comment: "From 1840 to 1960, every person elected to the Presidency of the United States in a year that ended with zero died in office. Therefore Reagan will not complete his term."

2. I have never seen a purple cow, so I never expect to see one.

3. Over the past one hundred years, no period of economic expansion has lasted more than seven years. Therefore we should expect a recession soon.

4. In my first-year class of thirty students, nobody knows the difference between a noun and a verb. I conclude that the present generation of students are illiterate about grammar.

5. "As there are men who make mistakes in reasoning even on the simplest topics in geometry, I judged that I was as liable to error as any other." R. Descartes, *Discourse on Method*.

6. "I saw that there was nothing at all in this statement, 'I think, therefore I am,' to assure me that I was saying the truth, unless it was that I saw very clearly that to think one must exist. So I judged that I could accept as a general rule that the things which we conceive very clearly and very distinctly are always true." R. Descartes, *Discourse on Method*.

7. "The broad facts remain. Life had progressed even before man was first evolved. Life progressed in giving rise to man. Man has progressed during the half-million or so years from the first Hominidae, even during the ten thousand years since the final amelioration of climate after

the Ice Age. And the potentialities of progress which are revealed, once his eyes have been opened to the evolutionary vista, are unlimited." J. Huxley, *Man in the Modern World*.

8. "**Socrates:** Then actions are performed according to their own nature, not according to our opinion. For instance, if we undertake to cut anything, ought we to cut it as we wish, and with whatever instrument we wish, or shall we, if we are willing to cut each thing in accordance with the nature of cutting and being cut, and with the natural instrument, succeed in cutting it, and do it rightly, whereas if we try to do it contrary to nature we shall fail and accomplish nothing?

"**Hermogenes:** I think the way is as you suggest.

"**Socrates:** Then, too, if we undertake to burn anything, we must burn not according to every opinion, but according to the right one? And that is as each thing naturally burns or is burned and with the natural instruments?

"**Hermogenes:** True.

"**Socrates:** And all other actions are to be performed in like manner?

"**Hermogenes:** Certainly." Plato, *Cratylus*.

9. "The earth is a middle-class planet, not a planet like Jupiter, nor yet one of the smaller vermin like the minor planets. The sun is a middling sort of star, not a giant like Capella but well above the lowest classes. So it seems wrong that we should happen to belong to an altogether exceptional galaxy. Frankly I do not believe it; it would be too much of a coincidence. I think that this relation of the Milky Way to the other galaxies is a subject on which more light will be thrown by further observational research, and that ultimately we shall find that there are many galaxies

of a size equal to and surpassing our own." A. Eddington, *The Expanding Universe*.

CHAPTER 5

STATISTICAL INDUCTION

When a farmer brings a truckload of wheat into the grain elevator to sell, the elevator operator reaches into the midst of the grain and takes out a handful. Then he counts the seeds to see how many of them are wild oats or other weeds, how many are undeveloped, and how many are of good quality. On the basis of his analysis, he offers the farmer a price for the shipment. He has drawn an inference from the handful, as a sample, about the whole truckload of wheat.

This, too, is an induction, but of a somewhat more complicated form. For it is not trying to identify a new characteristic (or targetted predicate) of the category of seeds, something that is found in all instances. It recognizes that both the sample and the population are collections of various kinds of seeds. And it proposes finding out the proportions of these different kinds in the population by counting the sample. Because proportions are involved, and they can be represented in percentages, we call this a statistical induction.

Here, as in simple inductions, there is a basic similarity between the sample and the population. In this example, they are from the category of seeds. But what is of interest now is the fact that there are a number of sub-categories: wheat, wild oats and other weeds, which are to be found in both sample and population. The induction assumes that the relationships between those sub-categories will be the same in the population as in the sample.

For a statistical induction to be successful, the sample must *adequately represent* the population. It is not sufficient that they be of the same category; they also must have the same mix of sub-categories. The elevator operator assumes that the grain has been so well stirred in being transferred from combine to granary to truck that there are no pockets of weed seeds, no concentrations of healthy wheat. If he is not sure, he stirs up the grain before taking his sample. One part should have the same proportions as any other.

When we say that the sample "represents" the population, we mean that the sample is like the population in any respects that might affect the induction. We are once again drawing an analogy. The adjusted argument form is:

Premise 1: The sample is like (or represents) the population because it has been selected in ways A to N.
Premise 2: The sample has the proportion A:B:C.
Conclusion: Therefore the population has the proportion A:B:C.

In our example:

Premise 1: The handful represents the population because it has been randomly selected from a well-mixed load of grain.
Premise 2: The handful has 10 wild oat seeds, 5 undeveloped wheat seeds and 35 healthy wheat seeds.
Conclusion: So 70% of the load is of good quality, 20% has weeds, and 10% are poor seeds.

In assessing this kind of induction, the crucial point must be how representative the sample is. Does it reflect the overall make-up of the population? Every statistical induction should indicate how the sample has been selected from the population. We then can evaluate whether that process of selection makes the sample representative.

In our example, the grain was well mixed (or at least the operator assumed that it was), and the action of the operator in grabbing his handful was not directed in any way, but was quite random. This seems sufficient to ensure that the induction was well based. The word "random" in that description is a technical term. A selection is made *randomly* when each member of the population has an equal chance of being selected.

However, not all statistical inductions are so easily justified.

Sociologists and market researchers use this kind of reasoning regularly. They select a sample of the people living in a province, region or country, and the percentages they obtain are extended to the population as a whole. If they are interested in marketing gasoline, it does not help to interview randomly only in a club for old age pensioners, or simply to intercept people in the mall of an affluent suburb. The general population of a country includes a wide variety of people: farmers, owners of small businesses, secretaries, shift workers, teachers, garbage collectors, unemployed, nurses and doctors, managers and executives of large firms, and so on. A sample that is not varied enough to capture some of that diversity will not provide a good basis for extending the statistical results of the sampling to the population as a whole.

Therefore those conducting surveys take steps to ensure that their sample is *representative*. In addition to the questions they ask about gasoline and car usage, for example, they ask other questions about gender, age, educational level, income level, and the type of community in which the person being interviewed lives. Then they "weight" their sample so that the proportions of women to men, of rich to poor, of city-dwellers to rural people are the same as those found in the population as a whole. For the statistics of the population in general they appeal to data provided by the regular census. If, for example, they have too many people whose income is from $20,000 to $40,000 they will randomly select just the appropriate number for the size of their final sample. But in doing so, they have to be sure that they do not alter the other proportions: of women to men, of farmers to suburbanites, of young people to pensioners, etc.

By making the sample representative with respect to the very general characteristics of gender, income, location of residence, and so on, the surveyor is ensuring that the sample is sufficiently like the population to make the inductive inference strong. In other words, the sample is representative.

A second consideration is important: the size of the sample must also be taken into account. Statisticians claim that a sample of eleven hundred is the minimum for a good statistical induction about the population of a country or region. That number is required to make sure that the sub-groups (such as young city-dwelling women earning over $40,000) are large enough to prevent individual idiosyncracies from affecting the calculation. If the eleven hundred are scattered representatively across the full range of the population, then the results should be fairly accurate.

Consider the following account by a social scientist in which he explains his sample:

Size and *representativeness* are the two key criteria in being able to generalize with accuracy from a sample to a population; considerable care, therefore, has been taken to ensure that both standards have been met. First, concerning size, an interest in provincial comparisons resulted in 1,917 cases being gathered in 1975; in 1980, the sample numbered 1,482; in 1985, 1,630.

Second, with respect to representativeness, the nation has been stratified by province (ten) and community size (greater than 100,000; 99,999-10,000; less than 10,000), with the sample drawn proportionate to the national population. As resources have improved, the number of communities involved has increased from thirty in 1975 to forty-three in 1980 to one hundred and four in 1985. Participants have been randomly selected using telephone directories (as of 1985 98.2% of Canadian households owned telephones). Discrepancies between the sample and population characteristics have been corrected by weighting (1975: province, community size, gender; 1980: those three variables as well as age; 1985: province, gender, age). Each of the three samples has been weighted down to about twelve hundred cases in order to minimize the use of large weight factors (i.e., three or more). [R.W. Bibby *Fragmented Gods*, (Toronto, 1987) 273f.]

Notice that Professor Bibby's procedure does not completely satisfy the standards of randomness. People who do not have phones and people who have unlisted numbers have no chance of being selected. While the number of communities considered has increased, there is no indication that they were randomly selected; so that inhabitants of some areas may have had less chance of being selected. In addition, since the questionnaire was mailed out, the sample included only those who were sufficiently responsible or conscientious to reply: from 52% to 65%. This did not bother Prof. Bibby: "I hold the somewhat unconventional view that return rate is not necessarily a critical issue if one can establish that a representative sample of sufficient size has been attained." [174] In other words, by making the sample representative, he holds that the flaws involved in not having a completely random selection are overcome.

All social sampling and market research falls short of the strict standard of randomness. In practice, especially when you are working with the total population of a country or a large region, it is impossible to give everyone a completely equal chance of being selected. This, of course, reduces the accuracy of the induction, and that is frequently reported in the statistical figures that talk about chances of error. Nonetheless, if care has been taken to make the sample representative, the results are sufficiently accurate to encourage politicians and business people to adapt their policies and products to meet the "market".

When assessing a statistical induction the first question focuses on the first premise. How does the researcher ensure that the sample is representative? She should be like Professor Bibby in weighting her count to counterbalance the unrandom elements in the selection. A full account of her method will include all the procedures used. By comparing the actual process of selection with the pure standard of randomness, one has some basis for deciding whether the statistical induction is well based or not.

Few people actually have the full accounts to read. They are given summaries in the popular press. As a result, it is frequently very difficult to be sure that the researcher was as responsible as Professor Bibby. Consider the following:

The Liberal Party still has a substantial lead over the Progressive Conservatives and the New Democratic Party, the latest Globe-Environics poll shows. The new poll shows the opposition Liberals with the support of 40% of decided voters, the New Democrats with 30% and the Conservatives with 29%. One per cent would vote for other parties. Only 15% of eligible voters say they are undecided about which party they would support in a federal election, compared with 18% who were undecided or refused to state a preference in the December poll. The survey was conducted by Environics Research Group Ltd. among a representative nationwide sample of one thousand nine hundred and eighty-three eligible voters from March 7 to 24. [*The Globe and Mail*, March 29, 1988, reprinted by permission of Environics Research Group Ltd.]

Since this is all that we are given, we have no way of knowing whether the sample was representative or not. We are being asked to trust the reporter or the person who wrote the press release for Environics Research Group Ltd. We have no evidence of the precautions taken to balance the fact that the selection was not random. And so we have no clear basis for assessing the accuracy of the induction. In practice, for informal purposes, we probably do not need all that data. The newspaper is simply purveying other people's press releases. But if we intend to base serious plans on the results we should investigate further.

There is, however, another consideration to take into account when we are evaluating a statistical induction. This concerns the second premise which tells us the various numbers or percentages found in the sample. Statistics always require two numbers, one of which is represented as a proportion of the other; that proportion is then converted to a percentage. (Number A is to number B as x is to 100). Whenever we run across statistics and percentages it is important to ask the question: what is proportional to what? What is the base set of numbers that is to provide the figure of 100, and what is the other set of numbers? And how were both of them determined?

If we are counting wild oat and wheat seeds, it is quite easy to know which is which (although I would rather trust someone with quite a bit of experience in harvesting and marketing grain). The 10 wild oat seeds (number A) are set against the total of fifty seeds in the sample (number B) to produce 20%.

But in the social sciences we are on much more difficult grounds. For in this case what is being counted is answers to questions. And to make sure that the answers can be organized easily into categories, the questions need to be framed so that there are only a limited number of answers. The person being interviewed has to be able to say: Yes or No. Or the questionnaire provides a five or seven point range from strongly yes to strongly no. At times, the investigator tries to limit the options by giving a choice of several answers.

Once again I will use the example of Reginald Bibby's surveys on the practice of religion in Canada.

Which of the following comes closest to your view of life after death?
— I believe that there must be something beyond death, but I have no idea what it may be like
— There is life after death, with rewards for some people and punishment for others

—I am unsure whether or not there is life after death
—I don't believe in life after death
—The notion of reincarnation expresses my view of what happens to people when they die
—There is life after death, but no punishment
—Other
[*Fragmented Gods*]

Bibby has spelled out possible answers to his question about life after death. Once he has counted the responses, he can draw his conclusions and say that 40% of the 1,298 people in his sample checked the first option. By combining positive answers to the first, second, fifth and sixth options, Bibby is able to draw the conclusion that "belief in life after death receives greater endorsement [than in Gallup polls], reaching about 65%." This then becomes the figure that he builds into his charts. To be able to count answers that can then be rendered as a percentage, he has asked his respondents to fit their beliefs and ideas into a fixed framework.

However, Bibby goes further. Not only does he ask his respondents whether they think of themselves as committed Christians, he uses his own calculations to decide whether they can be classified as committed in the traditional sense. He combines the appropriate answers to his questions about belief in God, in Jesus Christ and in life after death, together with some indication of regular prayer, reporting experiences of divine presence, and correct answers about who were Old Testament prophets and which disciple denied Jesus three times. The result is a set of respondents that Bibby calls "traditionally committed Christians."

Notice what Bibby has done. He has taken attitudes and practices that vary widely from individual to individual;

and he has sorted them into some kind of pattern that he can count. This process of taking a concept or notion (like "traditionally committed Christian") and translating it into countable features is called *operationalizing*. Bibby has *operationalized* "belief in life after death" as positive answers to four of his options. And he has operationalized "committed Christian" into the group who gave appropriate answers to eight specific questions.

In assessing his statistical induction, then, we need to be satisfied that the things he has actually counted—in this case the answers to the questions he has asked—do adequately represent the statements he makes about his sample: that 65% "believe in life after death"; that 35% of those who claimed they were committed to Christianity manifest in fact the characteristics of being "traditionally committed".

If surveyors do not, as Professor Bibby has done, spell out possible answers to their questions, they can run into trouble. In a study on *The Affluent Worker in the Class Structure* [Goldthorpe et al. Cambridge, 1969] interviewers were advised to follow "the natural flow of the discussion" and to "formulate their questions in ways consistent with what they had already learnt about respondents' ideas and conceptions." This information was then coded into slots that would allow counting. Any pattern of slots that seemed to pose serious problems—"where the average disagreement between coders was calculated at greater than 15%"—was abandoned. Nonetheless, because the researchers left slots where disagreement was 15% or less, it is clear that there was still considerable variation. What was counted under any one category would depend on who had done the coding.

Some of the tables that resulted from the survey suggest that this procedure did not solve all the problems. The table that identifies the images people had about class structure shows that 26% had images that did not fit the coding model of power/prestige/money, and 7% had "no communicable image." In other words, one third of the sample could not really be counted into the slots provided. At the same time, the three identifiable slots that survived the earlier screening ("power", "prestige", and "money") were not particularly sophisticated. And some of them do not seem to be particularly important either, for "power" garnered only 4% and "prestige" 8%; both considerably less than the 33% for the unassigned.

Thus when sociologists surrender their preformulated answers and allow their repondents to give natural responses, they have difficulty with the second premise in their inference. They do not have items that can easily be counted.

The second kind of assessment for a statistical induction, then, concerns the way in which the concepts used to describe the sample were operationalized so that they could be counted. It is clear that the kind of questions that can be asked on a questionnaire can never do justice to the subtleties of personal feelings and beliefs. We need to be satisfied that they are as appropriate as possible.

A statistical induction moves from a sample to a population in the same way that a categorical induction, or generalization, does. But it does not extend a simple targetted predicate to a category. It discovers that a set of predicates appear in a definite proportion in the sample and extends that ratio to the population as a whole. It usually expresses that proportion, or ratio, in terms of percentages.

Two factors need to be taken into account in assessing a statistical induction. In the first place we must discover how representative is the sample, and what degree of accuracy it provides for making an inference about the population.

In the second place, we need to consider the way in which the concepts used in the percentages and proportions have been operationalized. What kinds of things were counted to give the precise numbers? Are these things adequately reflected in what is being said about them?

Few statistical inductions in the social sciences are fully adequate by either of these criteria. This is frequently indicated by statisticians when they refer to a "margin of error". But this does not mean that they should simply be dismissed. The task of the assessor is to decide whether the procedures used will give results that are close enough to the ideal to be usable in practice.

Most statistical inductions are used as the bases for decisions in business and politics. The elevator operator decides how much he will pay for the grain; the church official decides how to tailor his message and his institutional practice to meet the needs of the modern world; the politician decides which policies to implement, and how to focus his campaign; the manufacturer decides how to advertise his products, and where to concentrate in developing new ones. Actions such as these cannot wait for precise and fully accurate statistics; the moment for decision passes too quickly. The question to ask of social sampling, then, is whether the results are sufficiently reliable that actions can be based on them. We cannot realistically expect more.

NOTE

We must be careful about percentages and statistics. Since one set of figures or percentages can be used as the base of 100 for another set, it can frequently become quite confusing and misleading. Therefore it is important to read carefully to notice what is a percentage of what.

For example, when we read in the business pages that the rate of inflation has increased by 5%, we may be inclined to think that the inflation rate is 5% — that is, a dress which cost $100 last year will cost $105 this year. But that is not what was said. The paper is rather reporting that the *inflation rate* this year is 5% greater than the *inflation rate* last year: if last year our dress went up 10% in price to $110, this year it is going up a further 10% plus 5% of 10%, making 10.5% in all. So the dress will cost $121.55. The base for the percentages is not the cost of goods last year, but the rate by which they increased in price last year.

Most of us are inclined to be overawed by numbers. And whenever we see percentages we stop thinking critically. But it is always important to ask: what is the base represented by the figure of 100 in the percentage? (Remember that "percent" means "for each hundred".) Once we get that clear, we will not as likely be misled by statistics.

EXERCISE A:

For each of the following statistical inductions, set it out in standard form, then specify what you know about the representativeness of the sample and about the way concepts were operationalized into countable items. Assess whether the results are sufficiently reliable.

Example: "The federal Liberal Party has moved into the lead over the Conservative Party, according to the latest poll done for The Globe and Mail by Environics Research Group Ltd.
"A total of 1,538 eligible voters were surveyed in two waves following last week's televised debates among the three party leaders, in French on Monday night and in English on Tuesday night.

"In the first wave, conducted last Tuesday and Wednesday nights, the Liberals moved into a dead heat with the Tories.

"By the weekend, however, continuing momentum raised the Liberals into a six-point lead with the support of 37 per cent of decided voters, compared with 31 per cent for the Conservatives and 26 per cent for the New Democratic Party; six per cent would vote for other parties. These figures were reached after calculations to eliminate the 13 per cent of the total voters sampled who were undecided or refused to state a preference.

"The margin of error on this wave of polling is plus or minus 3.6 percentage points in 19 out of 20 samples.

"On the basis of the current party standings, the Liberals would now have enough votes to form a minority government." Michael Adams, Donna Dasko and James Matsui, *The Globe and Mail National Edition*, November 1, 1988, reprinted with permission of Environics Research Group Ltd.

Standard form:

Premise 1: The sample of a portion of 1538 voters is like the population of all Canadian voters. [The figure of 1538 includes both those surveyed on Tuesday and Wednesday and those surveyed on the weekend.]
Premise 2: 37% of 87% of the sample said they would support the Liberal Party. [The 13% who had expressed no preference or refused to answer were eliminated before the percentages were determined.]
Conclusion: 37% of all those likely to vote in an election would have voted for the Liberal Party (and

that would have produced a minority Liberal government).

Assessment: Because the sample includes only a part of the 1538 voters, it is likely not large enough to be completely reliable. There is no information about how the sample was selected, so we cannot decide whether it was genuinely representative. (The reference to the statistical margin of error suggests that the sampling was in fact controlled.)

The questions asked of the sample were not reported; from the article one would assume that it went something like: "If the federal election were held today, for which party would you vote?" The count, then, is of people who *said* they would vote Liberal, not necessarily those who would in fact have voted Liberal. The connection is close enough, however, to suggest that the concept was appropriately operationalized.

One would need more information before being able to decide whether the results reported were reliable.

1. In the *CAUT Bulletin* of June 1988, Neil Guppy of the University of British Columbia reported on a national survey of postsecondary students conducted by Statistics Canada: "The 1983-84 data is based on questionnaire results from a sample of 45,181 students (an 85% response rate) and has been weighted to the size of population from which the sample is drawn."

On the basis of this survey, he reproduced a table of total postsecondary enrolment by sex and program:

[The following table is reprinted with permission of *CAUT Bulletin* and Neil Guppy.]

	% Female	Total Number
College Vocational, etc.	50.6	168,403
College University Credit	47.5	61,201
Undergraduate	47.8	319,450
Professional	49.1	22,435
Postgraduate	39.3	42,067
Total	48.1	613,555

2. "Although President Ronald Reagan has called the Soviet Union 'the evil empire,' it now is clear that he was not speaking for most Americans.

"New poll data show that 76 per cent of Americans like Soviet leader Mikhail Gorbachev and 59 per cent believe economic competitors like Japan pose more of a threat to their national security than traditional military adversaries like the Soviet Union.

"And when Americans were asked what should be the most important goal of their national security, the battle against international drug trafficking ranked first, well ahead of correcting the U.S. trade imbalance, countering Soviet aggression or fighting terrorism.

"The poll also shows that Americans no longer take for granted their position as the world's No. 1 economic power, and they believe that economic power is more important than military power in determining a country's influence in the world today....

"The new poll, a telephone survey of 1,004 voters taken in March, 1988, was conducted by four companies co-operating in a non-partisan project called Americans Talk Security, which has produced four comprehensive surveys of attitudes on national security issues in the last six months,

"The poll is considered accurate within 3.1 percentage points, 95 times out of 100." Stevie Cameron, *The Globe and Mail*, May 23, 1988. Reprinted with permission.

3. "If given a chance, most Americans would abandon their health care system and adopt something similar to the one in Canada, according to a survey of attitudes toward medical care in Canada, the United States and Britain....

"The survey was conducted by Louis Harris and Associates, a polling firm, for the Baxter Foundation of Deerfield, Ill., and published in its journal, the Health Management Quarterly. The foundation is the philanthropic arm of Baxter International, a U.S. health care company.

"The study was based on responses to identical questions put to 1,250 Americans, 1,026 Canadians and 1,667 Britons. It is considered accurate within five percentage points.

"Americans were found to be the most dissatisfied, with 89 per cent saying their health care system needed 'fundamental change or complete rebuilding,' compared with 69 per cent of the Britons and only 42 per cent of the Canadians, who were found the happiest of the respondents.

"Americans apparently are so frustrated and discouraged with their existing health care arrangements that 61 per cent say they would favor a system like that in place in Canada,' according to the survey." Martin Mittelstaedt, *The Globe and Mail*, February 14, 1989. Reprinted with permission.

4. "While 65 per cent of Ontario's university students are moderate drinkers, nearly 30 per cent are consuming 15 or

more drinks each week, says a major study undertaken by the Addiction Research Foundation.

"Among the biggest drinkers, 18 per cent are classed as heavy drinkers (15 to 28 drinks a week) and the more than 11 per cent who have more than 28 drinks a week are 'at risk,' the study says....

"Almost 5,000 full-time undergraduate students responded to the study, from a total of 13,200 randomly selected from four unidentified universities." Rita Daly, *The Toronto Star*, February 15, 1989. Reprinted with the permission of The Toronto Star Syndicate.

EXERCISE B:

Assess how samples were selected in the following sociological surveys and psychological experiments. If the selection indicates how a concept was operationalized, evaluate the operationalization.

EXAMPLE: A 1965 survey of the beliefs and attitudes of United Church people.
"To ensure representativeness, we chose 209 congregations at random, stratified first by region, defined by Conferences and Presbyteries [United Church regional divisions], and secondly by type of community. We defined as rural, concentrations of less than 5,000 persons, as towns, places having populations of between 5,000 and 32,000, and as cities, places having over 32,000 inhabitants. We kept market and industrial towns separate until it was evident that for our purposes there were no systematic differences between them. We were able to combine the midtown and downtown segments, as differences between them were slight in the variables we were interested in. We also found it possible to

combine returns from the eleven Conferences into four regions without serious distortion or loss of important data.

"The number of congregations drawn for the sample from each region and type of community was in the same proportion as the ratio of these sub-groups to each other in the entire church population, by reported numbers of members. Within each Conference the number of each type of congregation for the sample was decided on by weighting the total number of congregations by the average size of each type, determined by count of members.

"We wrote to ministers of a slightly greater than ideal sample of congregations, inviting their participation and requesting lists of members and adherents. The response was high. Distribution closely resembled the ideal sample. Replacement congregations were drawn at random within strata to complete the sample.

"Congregational lists were coded to show type of affiliation. We drew one name out of approximately thirty persons in each congregation. Cases were selected at random within six kinds of affiliation, each of which, we thought, would be approximately equal in size. We also chose an equal number of men and women. Returns were as follows: core members, 22 per cent of the actual sample; modal members and adherents, 31 per cent; inactive members, 9 percent; inactive adherents, 5 per cent; active youth, 27 per cent; inactive youth, 5 per cent; not known, 2 percent. The actual sample consisted of nearly 49 per cent men and over 51 per cent women.

"Two follow-up postcards were sent to non-respondents in four-week intervals in an attempt to maintain the sample by size and composition. Sixty per cent of all replies were received without reminders, 37 per cent after the first postcard and 3 per cent after the second. Differences between early and late responses were slight.

"Replies from laymen totalled 1,708, or 47 per cent of the 3,656 questionnaires mailed out. Ministers who completed individual questionnaires numbered 196 and General Council officers another 51. The actual sample of laymen approximated the ideal sample within two percent, by region and type of community...."

"Our concept of *urbanism* refers to a pattern or style of life rather than residence in an urban centre. Urbanism means openness to new ideas, heterogeneity in relations, a high rate of personal interaction, rationality in reaching decisions. It implies a pluralistic system of authority, high exposure to mass and other media of communication, specializing in work and high mobility rates." S. Crysdale, *The Changing Church in Canada*. Reprinted with permission.

Sample: *Size:* The number of laymen is large enough to ensure that idiosyncrasies are not given too heavy a weighting. The numbers for ministers and General Council officers are too small for adequate sampling.

Representativeness: The stratification of congregations by region and size of community, and the weighting to ensure that the proportions within the sample were the same as the proportions within the church as a whole serve to make the sample representative. Within each "strata" choice was random.

The choice of individuals also appears to have been both stratified and random, although one is not sure how the congregational lists were coded to determine core members, inactive adherents, etc.

Operationalization of "urbanism": The concepts listed that are grouped to define this term are abstract, and would be difficult to encode in a questionnaire. We are, however, not given information in this selection on how they were encoded.

1. Alison Gopnik investigated the relationship between young children's early use of the word *gone* and their development of the object concept.

"As part of a more general study of non-nominal words I recorded nine children's spontaneous uses of *gone*. The children were divided into three groups. Group I included three children who were audio-recorded in their homes for one hour every two weeks. The observer described the contexts of utterances on the audiotape. The children were first recorded when they were 12 months old and recording continued until they reached the two-word stage.... A group of six children were videotaped in their homes for a half hour every month for six months. Three of these children (Group II) were first recorded at 15 months, and three (Group III) were first recorded at 18 months. All the children were from the Oxford area. They came from middle-class and working-class backgrounds. The atmosphere during the recording sessions was informal and the children interacted with parents, siblings and the observer freely.

"A total of 378 utterances of *gone* were recorded. Each of the nine children used *gone* at one time or another.... *Gone* usually had a falling intonation, but occasionally children produced it with a rising intonation, usually as they looked quizzically at the experimenter after a particularly odd disappearance. The rising pattern seemed to reflect an interrogative speech act, rather than anything particularly relevant to the meaning of *gone*.

"I examined the contexts in which children used *gone*, in order to determine what concept *gone* encoded." A. Gopnik, "The acquisition of *gone* and the development of the object concept." *Journal of Child Language* (1984), published by Cambridge University Press. Reprinted with permission.

2. A study of the role of school superintendent:

"Consideration was at first given to using all the school superintendents in New England as the population. This idea was discarded when we discovered that there was considerable variability among the several states in the legal provisions for the position of school superintendent and school board member. In Connecticut, for example, the chief local school official in towns with a population less than 3500 is appointed by the State Department of Education, whereas in Massachusetts, the superintendent is always appointed by the local school board. It was felt advisable to control such 'state variables' since they might confound the substantive conclusions of the research. Since the number of superintendency positions in Massachusetts was considerably larger than in any other New England state, it was decided to specify all Massachusetts school superintendencies as the population. At one point consideration was given to the possibility of interviewing all 217 superintendents in Massachusetts. A later decision to conduct lengthy interviews precluded this more expansive and more expensive plan. But in view of the relatively small size of the population of the superintendents in Massachusetts, and in order to secure an adequate number of cases for purposes of analysis, the sample size was set at half the total number of superintendencies.

"To obtain the sample the following procedure was used. A list of all superintendency positions was obtained from the Massachusetts State Department of Education.

These 217 superintendencies were categorized on the basis of four geographical areas in order to eliminate any geographical bias in selecting the sample. The problem then was to obtain a 50 per cent random sample within each geographical area. Three stratification criteria were used in drawing subsamples from each of the geographical areas.

1. Whether it was a union or nonunion superintendency (a union superintendency is one in which the superintendent is in charge of two or more school systems).

2. The population of the community or communities for which the superintendent administered the local public education program.

3. The extent to which the community or communities gave financial support to the public schools relative to their ability to pay for it....

"The superintendencies in each geographical area were then paired according to their similarity with respect to these three criteria. Since there were 7 superintendencies which could not be paired by this process, 105 pairs, or 210 superintendencies, were left in the population. A coin was flipped to select the superintendency from each pair to be included in the sample. The resulting 105 superintendencies constitute the sample of the School Executive Studies.

"We were able to interview 102 of the superintendents in the sample. The 3 superintendents with whom interviews could not be arranged were replaced by their 'duplicates' in the matched sample, bringing the total number of superintendent interviews to 105." Gross, Mason and McEachern, *Explorations in Role Analysis*.

3. For a study of working class consciousness in Detroit:

"We interviewed only blue-collar workers with particular ethnic and regional backgrounds: those of German, British, Canadian, Polish, Ukrainian, and Negro descent were eligible for the interview. We excluded southern-born whites, since their ethnic background was different from that of other Anglo-Saxons and Germans.

"In order to choose the eligible, we traced the descent line through the respondent's father. Where this line was mixed, we selected the nationality group with the higher prestige; thus, if a respondent's father was German-Polish, we classified the respondent as German. Fortunately, only a small number of respondents claimed mixed nationality on their father's side....

"From each of the seven districts we drew separate samples. Unfortunately, the number of potential respondents chosen from each district depended in part upon the reception given the interviewers. We had to curtail interviewing in one ghetto area (District 2) after a gang chased one of the interviewers away. District 2 was not unique; in District 7 many respondents were exceedingly unco-operative. In spite of the general hostility of the respondents in this district, the interviewers attempted to complete the schedules.

"In another district (District 1), a very large proportion of potential respondents turned out to be members of white-collar occupations or ineligible ethnic groups. We therefore had to select a disproportionally large number of respondents from the district.

"The selection of the sample proved to be an on-going process. Our staff had originally planned to interview 100 respondents from each of the following clusters: (1) Negroes, (2) Poles and Ukrainians, and (3) Germans, Britons, and Canadians. At the same time, anticipating our statistical analysis, we had planned to include in each of the three clusters 50 respondents whose total personal income was less than $5000 in 1959. In the case of Negroes and Poles, this task did not prove to be a problem, since they were often in low-income brackets. Unfortunately, but expectedly, proportionally fewer Germans, Britons or Canadians earned less than $5000. It was therefore necessary to oversample the district where they were heavily concentrated until we had interviewed 50 respondents who made less than this sum.

"Another problem — this one on data validity — was the possibility of bias arising out of an interview in which the participants belonged to diverse and sometimes antagonistic ethnic groups. However, we avoided this whenever possible by having Negro staff members interview Negro respondents, and vice versa. We did this in order to minimize racial barriers to communication within this racially conscious community. Still, in many cases, we found it necessary to use white interviewers among Negro workmen. Interestingly, when we compared the Negro interviews obtained by both whites and Negroes, there seemed to be few, if any, differences in results....

"To compensate for the small sampling, we focused on particular segments of the working class — only male, manual workers found in certain ethnic groups, located beyond the core of the central city but within its outer boundary." John C. Leggett, *Class, Race, and Labor.* Published by Oxford University Press. Reprinted with permission.

4. An attempt to explain the emergence of grammar by looking at changes in children's use of single-word utterances in the period of time before they use syntax in their speech.

"The principal source of data is a diary record of my daughter, Allison, begun with the appearance of her first words at nine months and concluded with the use of sentences at 22 months.... No attempt was made to record every utterance; rather notes were made and examples of speech events recorded at weekly intervals. These notes were supplemented by four 40-minute video tape records made at intervals in which a substantive change had been observed in Allison's use of speech; the video records were made at ages 16 months, 3 weeks; 19 months, 2 weeks; 20 months, 3 weeks; and 22 months." Lois Bloom, *One Word at a Time*, reprinted with permission of Mouton de Gruyter. [In this case consider the population as all utterances during this period by Allison.]

5. "In order to assess Fijian and Sikh attitudes about their relations with others, we developed a formal questionnaire, which was administered in 1977-78 to 100 Sikh and 110 Fijian adult males. Because we were dealing with a rather sensitive area of life, we employed a Sikh and a Fijian to conduct the interviews in the two respective communities.

"Methodological difficulties precluded the development of a specifically random sample of the Fijian and Sikh populations of the Vancouver area. [Note: We used a random sample of individuals with recognizably Sikh names derived from a local South Asian telephone directory to develop a list of Sikh respondents. The Fijian sample was drawn from a list developed by one of us (N. Buchignani)

TABLE 2
Sikh and Fijian Perceptions of Discrimination

Experience Discrimination	Sikhs		Fijians	
	%	Number	%	Number
Frequently	45.4	45	19.1	21
Occasionally	35.1	34	25.5	28
Rarely or Never	18.5	18	55.4	61
Total	100.0	97	100.0	110

during fieldwork in the Fijian community.] Nevertheless, comparison of the demographic data that were collected on age, occupation and marital status with Canada Employment and Immigration Statistics showed that our samples were quite representative. But, what is really of consequence for our argument here is that we developed two sample populations that were closely comparable....

"Perceived threat and conflict are difficult concepts to cover in a survey, for they are fairly abstract ideas. We chose to focus more narrowly on Sikh and Fijian perceptions of discrimination and upon Sikh and Fijian notions of where they and other immigrant groups fit into the Canadian society.

"The differences are striking indeed. Consider the responses [in Table 2] to a question about the frequency with which individuals experienced discrimination.

"Sikh and Fijian responses were almost directly opposite. These differences were not explainable as being functions of age, time of residence, type of occupation, marital status, or differential sensitivity to different types of discrimination. Ethnicity was the key variable." N. Buchignani and D. Indra, "Inter-group Conflict and Community Solidarity: Sikhs and South Asian Fijians in Vancouver," From the *Canadian Journal of Anthropology/Revue Canadienne d'Anthropologie*, Volume 1, No. 2, Winter 1980: 149-157. Reprinted with permission.

CHAPTER 6

CORRELATION

It took a long time to discover the connection between bacteria and disease. One of the early bits of evidence for the connection came in a 1837 report by Doctor Schwann:

Boil meat thoroughly and put it in a clean bottle and lead air into it that has passed through red-hot pipes—the meat will remain perfectly fresh for months. But in a day or two after you remove the stopper and let in ordinary air, with its little animals, the meat will begin to smell dreadfully; it will teem with wriggling, cavorting creatures a thousand times smaller than a pinhead. It is these beasts that make meat go bad. [Paul de Kruif, *Microbe Hunters*, 61]

At about the same time Cagniard de la Tour observed that no brew of hops or barley ever changed into beer without the presence of yeasts.

Both Schwann and de la Tour drew an inductive inference. They assumed that all meat, and all beer had the characteristics that they had noticed in their particular observations. Their experiments involved samples which were then extended to a general population.

But what is distinctive about their reasoning was the nature of the sample they used. While the meat and brew were chosen randomly, and the experiments were repeated, no serious attention was given to the way in which the samples represented the total population. That was not necessary. For in each of the experiments, *two* samples were used. In one the meat was enclosed in a clean bottle, or the brew was kept free from yeast; in the other ordinary air had contact with the meat, or yeast with the brew. The induction required that the two samples be as alike as possible except for the kind of air allowed in contact — or whether yeast was present or no. Because they were alike, the different results could come only from the differences introduced by the experimenters.

For these investigators were not interested in proportions: the ratio of fresh meat to putrid meat; of hops that became beer to hops that did not. They were after something else. They were looking to see if becoming putrid was connected with ordinary air; if fermentation was connected with yeast. In other words, each of them had two differences in mind: fresh/putrid and sterilized air/ordinary air; unalcoholic brew/beer and yeast/no yeast. The fresh meat was always found when only sterilized air came in contact with it; putrid meat had sat in ordinary air. Fermentation took place when yeast was present; nothing happened otherwise. It was the relation between the two differences that was in question. And since the differences are related to each other, we call it a *correlation*.

In a correlation, one of the differences is taken as basic; it is used to distinguish the two samples. One bit of meat is in sterilized air, the other in ordinary air; one brew is maintained (probably in sterilized air) without yeast, the other with yeast. Then the investigator looks to see whether the other difference (fresh/putrid, or alcoholic/non-alcoholic) follows a similar pattern. This gives a definite order to the two distinctions. The one that is used initially to differentiate the samples provides the *primary difference*; the other that is observed or discovered we call the *secondary difference*.

Quite often the primary difference is one that occurs naturally. Some people are older than others; women are distinct from men. However, in our examples the primary difference between the samples has been introduced by the investigator. For those experiments a further bit of technical vocabulary is used. The sample that has the difference added is called the *experimental group*; the one that is left alone is called the *control group*.

Correlations are a form of inductive reasoning. Like the previous forms of induction, they involve an analogy between samples and populations; they require careful sample selection; and the concepts to be investigated must be operationalized so that they can be counted. In one important sense, however, they are different. For what is to be generalized are the correlated *differences* between the two samples. When, in a properly controlled setting, the primary difference matches a secondary difference, an induction is warranted: the correlation is not limited to the samples, but applies generally.

We have been talking about the items correlated as differences. One kind of difference contrasts the presence with the absence of a factor. Since there are two differences in any correlation, presence can be related with absence in two ways. In one case, the presence of one factor is conjoined with the presence of the other. This is a *positive* correlation. Thus yeast is positively correlated with fermentation. In the other case, the presence of one factor is conjoined with the absence of the other. This is called a *negative* correlation. For example, fresh meat is negatively correlated with ordinary air.

The clearest cases are when the two samples are differentiated by complete presence and complete absence of both factors. But that is not always possible. And so investigators once again appeal to statistics. Significantly higher or lower percentages suggest differences sufficiently important that they can be correlated. If one set of percentages varies between the samples *at a similar rate* to the other set of percentages, then we say that they are correlated according to a *concomitant variation*.

In such a correlation the relation between the two factors must be quite regular. The secondary difference should vary (either positively or negatively) at the same rate as the primary difference. Where there is no pattern at all, the two differences simply cannot be correlated.

To be sure that the variation is consistent and reliable, we need more than two samples. Percentages based on samples are notoriously risky, since the sample may not be entirely random and it is frequently difficult to "control" the groups. Having three or more samples, differentiated according to a primary set of percentages, compensates for the fact that we are working with proportions rather than with complete presence or absence.

Concomitant variation is regularly used in sociological and psychological studies where the people being studied cannot be manipulated to separate samples in a clearcut way. For example, in a study conducted in the United Church of Canada during the 1960s, the mailed survey had one set of questions that together operationalized "urbanism" and another set of questions that rated people on whether they espoused a conservative or a liberal theology. The results were then put on a scale:

TABLE III-1
Liberal Theology of Laymen by Urbanism
(percentages)

Urbanism:	Low	Medium	High
Liberal Theology	38	45	66
(Number of Cases)	(452)	(1,010)	(243)

Explanation: Of the total sample of 1,705 laymen, 452 were found, by scoring certain attributes, to be low in the urban style of life, 1,010 were medium in urbanism and 243 were high. Of the 452 with low urbanism, 38 percent were liberal in theology; of the 1,010 persons with medium urbanism, 45 percent were theologically liberal; and of the 243 who were high in urbanism, 66 percent were liberal in their theology.
[S. Crysdale, *The Changing Church in Canada.* Reprinted with permission.]

In this case, there are three samples being compared. They have been taken from the total group surveyed, and the primary difference that distinguishes them is the degree of "urbanism" (as operationalized by the researcher). That difference is then correlated with the percentage of each sample that espouses "liberal" theology (another operationalized concept).

Crysdale has observed a concomitant variation. From this he draws the conclusion: "For social researchers this approaches a classical statistical correlation." Because a higher percentage of people scaled as high in urbanism had adopted a liberal theology, whereas people scoring low in urbanism were less likely to be liberal, urbanism could be said to be positively correlated with liberalism.

When an induction takes a correlation rather than a simple proportion for its targetted predicate, the method of assessment changes. A correlation requires more than one sample. And those samples are to be distinguished in terms of the primary difference. However, they are to be otherwise as similar as possible. If they are not basically alike, then there may well be other factors, not noticed, that affect the apparent correlation, and the results of the study cannot legitimately be extended to the population as a whole.

Here we have once again that combination of similarity and difference that is characteristic of analogies. The samples are to be *similar* in the key respects used in selecting them **except for** the *primary difference* that distinguishes the two or more samples. The more similar they are, the more reliable the induction from sample to population. Thus, the meat that remains fresh must be similar to the meat that putrifies in all respects other than the kind of air it contacts. The hops and barley that ferment should be no different at the beginning from those that do not. The only difference in question is to be the difference used to separate the two samples.

We can, however, strengthen the inference in another way. We may take other pairs or triads of samples that are quite different from our original set (making sure that within each set the samples are similar to each other). We then distinguish the pairs or triads, applying the same primary difference that we used in our original correlation. Instead of hops and barley, we try wheat, oats, or even cheese and see whether yeast turns out to be correlated with its fermentation. We expose milk or eggs, instead of meat, to both sterilized and unsterilized air and look for decay. We thus arrange further experiments with quite different kinds of samples. The greater the difference in kind between the sets of samples (provided that the primary difference continues to be correlated with the secondary difference), the stronger the inference to the population as a whole.

Any effective correlation involves both agreement and disagreement. If we have only one set of samples, the samples need to "agree" in key respects other than the "disagreement" used to differentiate them: meat from the same cut should be exposed to the different kinds of air. If we have more than one set, the sets should "disagree" in important ways other than their "agreement" about the primary difference: cheese as a dairy product differs considerably from grain, even though yeast is also used in its ripening. Where agreement and disagreement are carefully controlled, it is not necessary for the samples to be in fact representative of the total population. Researchers simply need to pair similar individuals between their two sample sets, or choose them at random from a pool of similar people or things. Then they try to "replicate" or repeat the same experiment using a totally different collection of individuals — from a different country, perhaps, or a different social class.

Where it is not possible to ensure that the various samples in a set are significantly similar, other techniques are required. In the example from Crysdale's book, mentioned above, Crysdale was not able to ensure that the three samples were significantly similar apart from the difference in urbanism, for he simply divided up the overall sample from his survey. Because of this limitation on the requirement of similarity, it was important that his overall sample be representative of his total population.

In other words, where agreement and disagreement cannot be controlled, and we are left with a concomitant variation, the standards of assessment revert to a criterion discussed in the last chapter for statistical induction: the sample must be representative.

Because a correlation is an induction, the other criterion also applies, for the numbers used to determine percentages involve some operationalizing of concepts. What in fact was Crysdale counting when he was deciding who were highly urbanized and who had adopted a liberal theology?

Correlation involves two differences or proportions; one of them is used initially to distinguish paired samples; the other is then observed among the samples. Where the two vary in a coordinated and regular way, we say that two factors are correlated. If both features are present (or simply stronger) in one sample and absent (or weaker) in the other, the correlation is a positive one. Where they are inversely related (presence with absence, or weaker with stronger), the correlation is negative. Where no regular pattern is observed no correlation can be claimed at all.

Correlations found in samples are inductively extended to populations. Such inferences are strong where the samples are similar in all key respects except for the one used to distinguish them. They are strengthened further whenever the same correlation has been found in sets of samples that are otherwise quite different from each other.

Since correlations are inductions, they are also to be assessed using the criteria applied to statistical inductions. Where sets of samples cannot be rigorously controlled in terms of agreement and disagreement, they need to be as representative as possible. If percentages and proportions are used, the operationalizing of concepts needs to be evaluated.

Notice that in this section we have been careful to talk about correlation, and not about causes. The move from correlation to cause is a distinct inference. For a correlation between differences does not tell us that the primary feature always *leads to* or *causes* the presence or absence of the secondary one. Sometimes we do want to say that the primary difference causes the secondary difference: that yeast causes fermentation. Sometimes we may want to suggest that the secondary difference causes the primary difference: that the adoption of liberal theology leads to greater urbanization. Sometimes we may want to say that there is a cause which is independent of both: it is not the ordinary air that causes putrefaction in the meat, nor the putrifaction that does anything to ordinary air, but bacteria, carried in the air, are the cause of the correlation. And sometimes, the correlation may be simply a coincidence that has no causal significance. Establishing a correlation between two factors, particularly in cases where the two samples cannot be rigorously controlled for agreement and disagreement, does not directly lead to any single inference about cause.

This is the point made by the tobacco industry about the relation between nicotine and cancer. While a positive correlation has been documented between smoking and lung cancer, the cigarette manufacturers stress that the causal linkage has not been established. Causes are something quite different from correlations.

So we must be cautious in assessing reports of scientific experiments. Quite frequently reporters and experimenters move directly from correlation to cause; because two kinds of things are regularly found together, they assume that one of them brings about or generates the other. They introduce causal language into the account. But a few minutes' thought should remind us that constant conjunction does not necessarily mean cause and effect; there are other possible explanations. To establish a causal link we need to look at a quite different kind of reasoning, which we call reasoning to explanation.

EXERCISE:

In each of the following correlations: (1) Identify a) the primary difference used to separate samples in the experiments, and b) the secondary difference discovered. (2) Assess the inductive inference a) by checking the way the samples have been selected, and b) by considering the way concepts have been operationalized. (3) Note if causal language has been introduced into the correlation.

EXAMPLE: "Since marginal working-class conflict occurs simultaneously along class and racial lines, certain aspects of *class* consciousness can be correlated with *racial* awareness.... We used a set of eight questions originally to measure class verbalization. We recoded the material in order to gauge the extent to which workmen used racial terms spontaneously in their replies. Subsequent analysis showed that the answers did demonstrate racial (or class-racial) awareness....

"If a workman used one (or more) racial terms when replying to the eight questions, he was coded as engaging in racial verbalization. We then related this to class verbalization. Class and racial consciousness were, in many cases, interrelated; when one occurred, the other did as well (see Table 6-1)

Table 6-1
Race of Worker and use of Racial and Class Symbols

Symbols	Negro (N = 120)	White (N = 255)
Use neither racial or class symbols (N = 50)	4%	18%
Use racial symbols only (N = 27)	7%	7%
Use class symbols only (N = 153)	38%	42%
Use both racial and class symbols (N = 145)	51%	33%

TOTAL = 375

NOTE: N refers to the number of cases

John C. Leggett, *Class, Race, and Labor.* Published by Oxford University Press. Reprinted with permission.

Primary and secondary difference: Despite the text, the samples in the table were separated not by whether they were class-conscious or not but along racial lines: between negro and white respondents. The secondary difference was then whether they used racial and class symbols separately, together, or not at all. On this basis one can say that negroes are more inclined to use both class and racial symbols; while whites are more inclined to use class symbols only. But the correlation is not strong.

However, the figures provided are enough to establish a measure of correlation between the use of class symbols (as the primary difference) and the use of racial symbols (as the secondary one). Using the information provided we can calculate that 107 negros and 191 whites used class symbols; 13 and 64 did not. 49% of the 298 who used class symbols also used racial symbols; 34% of the 77 who did not use class symbols used racial symbols. This suggests some measure of concomitant variation, although the sample size of 77 is quite small in comparison.

Sample: We do not know how the samples were selected, and whether the 255 whites were similar in other respects to the 120 blacks. Were they alike in age, occupation, education level? The selection does not tell us (although the full text might well provide that information — see Exercise 3 in the previous chapter).

Operationalization: The concepts "racial awareness" and "class consciousness" were operationalized by checking the answers to eight questions on other matters to see whether racial or class terms had been spontaneously used. We are not told what those questions were about. The fact that those interviewed did use such language does suggest that they are conscious of racial and class differences.

Causal language: No causal language is used.

1. "Table 3 presents the data concerning the relationship between [the use of the word] *gone* and the object-concept tasks. These findings support the suggestion that children acquire the word *gone* after they solve invisible displacement tasks (Task 13) and before they solve complex serial invisible displacement tasks (Tasks 14 and 15). All of the six children who did not solve Task 13 did not say *gone*. All but one of the nine children who solved Task 14 did say *gone*. In the intermediate group, children who solved Task 13 but did not solve Task 14, five said *gone* and four did not say *gone*. Three children not only solved Task 14 but also solved Task 15. All three of these children said *gone*.

Table 3
*Number of subjects at three different object-concept levels
and their use of gone*

| | Object-Concept Level | | |
LANGUAGE	< 13	= 13	> 13
Not using *gone*	6	4	1
Using *gone*	0	5	8

A.Gopnik & A. Meltzoff, "Semantic and cognitive development in 15- to 21-month-old children," *Journal of Child Language* (1984), published by Cambridge University Press. Reprinted with permission.

2. "The nature of the audience for religious programs is further clarified when the sample is analysed by age. Almost 80% of the regular audience are 55 or over; conversely, almost 90% of those who never watch such programs are under 55, more than half are under 35 (see TABLE 2.5)

Table 2.5
Religious Program Viewing by Age (In %)

RELIGIOUS TV VIEWING	AGE			
	18-34	35-54	55+	Total
Regularly (N=44)	4	17	79	100
Sometimes (N=183)	18	33	49	100
Seldom (N=309)	38	37	25	100
Never (N=641)	54	32	14	100

R. Bibby, *Fragmented Gods*.

(Note in this passage that the percentages are arranged horizontally and not vertically.)

3. "Psychologist Judith H. Langlois and colleagues (of the University of Texas at Austin) showed 34 infants pairs of women's faces, judged by adults as moderately attractive or unattractive. Half the pairs contrasted an attractive face with an unattractive one; the other half presented faces that were more alike, either attractive or unattractive.

"Since the infants, aged 6 to 8 months, could not tell the researchers which faces they preferred, Langlois and colleagues measured the amount of time they spent looking at each one. They also rated the attractiveness of each infant's mother, to see if the mothers' looks would influence their babies' preferences.

"The researchers found that the babies looked longer at attractive faces than at unattractive ones, regardless of their mothers' looks. Seventy-one percent looked longer at the attractive faces in the contrasting pairs, while 62 percent gazed longer at attractive pairs of faces than at unattractive ones.

"When the researchers repeated the experiment with 30 younger infants, aged 2 to 3 months, the mothers' attractiveness again had no effect. Almost two-thirds of these babies stared longer at attractive faces when paired with unattractive ones. However, when the faces were presented in like pairs, the infants did not look any longer at attractive faces than at unattractive ones." *Psychology Today*, August 1987, Reprinted with permission from *Psychology Today* magazine, Copyright c 1987 (PT Partners, L.P.).

4. "Another instance of how pervasive the indirect influence of the machine has been may be introduced here.... This concerns the theory of economic determinism. The increased productivity of our technology and the accompanying complexity of economic organization have resulted in a corresponding increase in the interdependence of individuals and communities. But it was just when the industrial revolution was at its height, and the economic problems presented by it had attained an order of difficulty perhaps never before experienced, that this theory in its present form was developed. It seems, therefore, that there might well be a discernible relationship between a point of view that holds economic phenomena to be basic in shaping other aspects of life and the historical setting of the period during which this concept was developed.

"There can be little doubt that economic factors do play an important part in influencing non-economic aspects of culture; but this merely recognizes the fact that all phases of life are closely interrelated and, because of this, tend to modify each other. In these terms, ours is by no means the only culture where economic factors are preponderant in influencing the other facets of culture. Yet it does remain an historic fact that it was only among a people — ourselves — whose economy had become more complex than any before experienced by man, and at a time when the problems presented by the economic order were becoming most serious, that this theory made its appearance." M.J. Herskovits, *Economic Anthropology*.

5. "Many of the most famous finds of fossil man have been marred by doubt as to the genuineness of bones.... If there were a reliable time-keeping mineral in bones such problems might be solved. Carnot, a French mineralogist, analysed a large number of bones from different geological horizons, and showed that their average fluorine-content increased with geological age.... Taking the proportion of fluorine to phosphate of lime in fluorapatite as unity, Carnot showed that the average proportion in bones of increasing age was as follows:

Recent	0.058
Pleistocene	0.360
Late Tertiary	0.595
Early Tertiary	0.645
Mesozoic	0.907
Paleozoic	0.993

Kenneth P. Oakley, "Fluorine and the Relative Dating of Bones," *The Advancement of Science* (1946), published by the British Association for the Advancement of Science. Reprinted with permission.

CHAPTER 7

ARGUMENT TO EXPLANATION

The sociologist Max Weber drew people's attention to an interesting correlation.

A glance at the occupational statistics of any country of mixed religious composition brings to light with remarkable frequency a situation which has several times provoked discussion in the Catholic press and literature, and in Catholic congresses in Germany, namely, the fact that business leaders and owners of capital, as well as the higher grades of skilled labour, and even more the higher technically and commercially trained personnel of modern enterprises, are overwhelmingly Protestant. This is true not only in cases where the difference in religion coincides with one of nationality, and thus of cultural development, as in Eastern Germany between Germans and Poles. The same thing is shown in the figures of religious affiliation almost wherever capitalism, at the time of its great expansion, has had a free hand to alter the social distribution of the population in accordance with its needs, and to determine its occupational structure. [M. Weber, *The Protestant Ethic and the Spirit of Capitalism*]

Given this positive correlation between being Protestant and being capitalist, Weber then asked: "Why were the districts of highest economic development at the same time particularly favourable to a revolution in the Church?"

In asking 'why' Weber was looking for an explanation of the correlation. Was it that cultures in which people were prepared to take economic initiatives more easily adopted the reformed faith? Was it that the Lutheran revolt encouraged people to venture boldly in the economic realm? Did capitalism cause the Protestantism, or Protestantism the capitalism? Or are both alternatives wrong? Was it a basic tendency towards personal independence and individualism that caused the adoption of both capitalism and Protestantism?

Notice that a correlation does not, of itself, imply any relationship or direction between the features correlated. It is simply a regular pattern. To find causes in correlations, or to claim some other reason for them, one needs to make further inferences — to an explanation.

In proposing his explanation, Weber went back to a particular idea introduced by Martin Luther in his interpretation of Christianity. That was the conception of labour or work as a calling, or vocation. This belief, Weber claimed, motivated the early Protestants to work with thorough conscientiousness, even though their rewards were meagre. The sense of labour being of value on its own provided in turn the foundation for capitalism.

In asking his question and proposing his answer, Weber was using a distinctive type of reasoning. Here he made no inductive generalization, going from sample to population. Nor did he simply notice a correlation. He was moving from a set of facts to an explanation of those facts. He was looking for an answer to the question: why are things just this way — why are capitalism and Protestantism correlated positively?

Causes are one form of explanation. Causes produce results. And if we know what produced a state of affairs, we have some idea why things are the way they are. Indeed, many people equate explanation with cause. If you give a cause and show how something has been brought about, you have explained it.

But there are other kinds of explanations as well. A mathematician wonders why we can test additions, subtractions, multiplications and divisions by the method of nines.

According to this method, you take any number, no matter how long; you add the digits of the number; and whenever you come to nine, you start again. In addition, for example, when you do this with each number to be added and then use the same procedure in adding the results together, the figure remaining will be exactly the same as the number you get when you follow the method of nines with the calculated total of the original addition. This is the short way of checking additions that many of us learned at school.

The mathematician finds this fact about the number nine curious. When he asks for an explanation of it, he is not asking about a cause, but about the mathematical *principles* from which one could deduce, or logically infer, this phenomenon. And he finds it in the fact that our number system is decimal, based on multiples of ten.

In a similar way, in their monumental work *Principia Mathematica*, Bertrand Russell and Alfred North Whitehead endeavoured to explain all of mathematics by tracing it back to its ultimate first principles.

A third kind of explanation attempts to fit a number of different facts into a single, coherent picture. In Conan Doyle's classic detective story, "The Speckled Band," we are told how Sherlock Holmes notices a number of details: the second half of a return ticket in the palm of his visitor's left glove; the left arm of her jacket spattered with fresh mud in no less than seven places. He puts these facts together to reach the explanation that Miss Stoner had started early to catch the train, and had a good drive in a dog-cart along heavy roads before reaching the station. He has explained why a set of curious facts are just the way they are.

A similar kind of inference occurs when Holmes puts the details of his client's story together with his investigations into her mother's will and his observations of the room where her sister died. Taking all the many details into account, he infers an explanation and anticipates the solution. Only then is he ready to set up the experiment that will establish its truth.

In each of these cases we have an argument to an explanation. Some set of facts attracts our curiosity. For Weber and the mathematician, there is an interesting regularity. For Sherlock Holmes and Miss Stoner there is something unusual and irregular. This provides the basis of the inference. And the conclusion is what we have called an explanation: a way of interpreting the facts so that they fit together, not only among themselves, but also with our wider experience and expectations.

The pattern for such reasoning looks like this:

Premise 1: Situation S has facts F^1, F^2, F^3...F^n.
Sub-conclusion: Explanation E would combine F^1, F^2, F^3...F^n into a single, integrated pattern. (In other words, they can be made to fit together.)
Conclusion: So E serves as an explanation for S.

The critical point in the argument is the move from premise 1 to the sub-conclusion. How do we arrive at E? For all that Sherlock Holmes calls his "deductions" elementary, this kind of reasoning is neither deductive nor obvious.

Those who have looked at this kind of reasoning in the past do not give us much help. Aristotle talks about quick wits, and C.S. Peirce calls it guessing.

The first thing to notice is the task which an explanation is meant to fulfill. It is to combine facts or observations into a single, integrated pattern. Once the concept of calling or vocation is introduced, for example, the correlation between Protestantism and capitalism makes sense. The decimal system of numbers removes the puzzle of the method of nines. And the hypothesis of a poisonous snake fitted with all the curiosities that Holmes had noticed.

It is not easy to spell out what we mean when we talk about a fit, or about a "single, integrated pattern". This is certainly not a question of correlation, of things being found next to each other in space, or simultaneous in time. For as we have seen, while correlations set the problems, they do not provide the explanations. Inferences to cause, to principle and to solution start from just those regularities (or irregularities) that generated the initial question. The explanation is to add something else. It is to arrange all the variety of facts in a single framework of meaning. It is to find a way of relating them. Each detail contributes to and acquires its significance from the total picture. The explanation is, in the first instance, not another fact, but a way of *understanding* facts, a way of *thinking about* them. And it relies on many different connections of meaning — on a network of relations.

For an explanation to work in the sub-conclusion, then, it must appeal to networks of meaning that are already familiar. Our experience offers a wide range of possibilities. The task in arguing to an explanation is to dredge up from our memory some possible relations that we might be able to transfer to our puzzling facts. Weber was already familiar with Luther's theology. If this were a totally new field, he could discover it by studying Luther's writing, and the statements of the Lutheran churches. What was not part of his own experience could be found in the experience of the culture. In his explanation, he applied one part of this to the framework of capitalism. And we suspect he focused on this part because he knew committed individuals whose diligent work achieved material success. He drew an analogy from his experience to the problem with which he was faced.

Holmes' encyclopaedic knowledge about snakes and India, milk and whipcords, among other things, was transferred to his particular problem in a similar way. It provided links between the puzzling facts.

We have already noticed that we use analogy to identify relations. In these inferences the investigators are searching for appropriate analogies that might provide bridges to possible explanations. They are looking for a pattern of relations that will enable the various facts to fit together and make sense.

So we can add another line to the pattern for our reasoning:

Premise 1: Situation S has facts F^1, F^2, F^3...F^n.
Premise 2: Analogue A relates items I^1, I^2, I^3...I^n, and these are similar to the facts in S.
Sub-conclusion: So explanation E (which is what A would look like in situation S) would combine F^1, F^2, F^3...F^n into a single, integrated pattern.

These features of an explanation do not make it any easier to reach a solution at the point where we are faced with an explanatory puzzle.[1] For in our experience and the

1 Although William J. McGuire, at the 1988 meeting of the Canadian Psychological Association, offered 49 tactics for generating hypotheses: "First catch your rabbit: Tactical heuristics for generating hypotheses in psychological research."

experience of our culture, we have many possible networks of relations upon which we could call. Many of them will turn out to be irrelevant and others will help only if they are considered from just the appropriate angle. The problem we face is how to find the needle in the haystack — the right explanation among all the possibilities.

However, the analysis we have provided so far does suggest some ways of assessing arguments to explanation. If we use these criteria of assessment to reject a number of possibilities, we can then focus on the few that should be taken seriously.

1. In the first place, an explanation needs to do justice to all the facts. It cannot ignore some, simply because they are inconvenient or difficult.

A great many explanations do not satisfy this requirement. Frequently reasoners do not find a solution to handle all the features of a puzzle, so they fall back on a proposal that fits only some of them and simply disregard the others, or ascribe them to unknown and perverse influences. It is not easy to find completely satisfactory explanations, and we often have to retreat to half-way measures of this sort. Nonetheless, whenever we do not integrate all the puzzling features into a single picture, we have not fully satisfied the requirements of an argument to explanation.

This criterion is regularly used for rejecting incomplete and inadequate proposals. This is illustrated in the way detectives in novels spell out the course of their investigations. Sherlock Holmes starts out being misled by the presence of gypsies and the murdered girl's cry of "speckled band". But he rejects the possibility of gypsies committing the crime once he sees that no gypsy could enter the room either through the window or through the door. His first explanation is set aside when it cannot fit all of the facts.

Many arguments for explanations concentrate on refuting alternative possibilities, using this criterion. They show that, in the proposal they are rejecting, some facts have not been sufficiently taken into account. By discarding options in this way, they make more plausible the theory they are advancing, since it alone does justice to the facts considered. However, they cannot establish it as the only possible explanation. For there may be some other way of combining the puzzling facts into a single picture that they have not yet considered.

(The application of this criterion is frequently complicated by the way in which people handle awkward facts. As we have seen, facts can be disregarded or ascribed to outside interference. In consequence, a debate between people with differing hypotheses may have difficulty finding common ground because one side takes seriously a set of facts dismissed by their opponents, while ignoring the facts they stress.)

2. The second criterion to take into account in assessing an argument of this sort is what people have called "simplicity." By that they mean that the explanation should appeal to analogues in our experience that relate items in a fairly straightforward way; that we must not create artificial and peculiar connections between ideas and features just to make the explanation work.

Julian Huxley makes this point about the battle over astronomy in the sixteenth century: "Even after Copernicus, the doctrine that the sun goes around the earth could still be logically maintained. But it demanded enormous complexity of epicycle upon epicycle. The rival theory that the earth goes around the sun was far simpler and more satisfying."

In one sense, the traditional theory was more familiar. Scholars had learned it when they were young, and the rhythm of sunrise and sunset suggested that the earth was stable and the sun moved. But it was not simpler. To do justice to the facts astronomers progressively learned about the location of the sun and the planets, the theory that they revolved around the earth had to be made more and more intricate and complex.

Even though we may have to think hard before coming up with a good explanation, then, it should not be artificial. We find reaching an explanation difficult, not because the connections to be discovered are complicated, but because we have never associated some of the relations that turn out to be successful with this puzzling set of facts. We need to cast around in our accumulated experience to discover a pattern that we can then transfer to this new and different context.

The appeal to simplicity takes us back to analogy. For an analogy identifies relations quite apart from the particular things they relate. An explanation offers a simple relation because we recall an analogy from somewhere else in our experience. Testing explanations against the criterion of simplicity and the operation of drawing analogies are close cousins.

The two criteria for the assessment of an argument to explanation, then, are that it should explain all the facts in question, all of F^1, F^2, F^3...F^n; and that it should be simple in the sense that it draws on a fairly clearcut pattern of relations present in accumulated experience.

These two frequently come into conflict. A simple explanation may be achieved by being cavalier with facts; too scrupulous attention to facts can complicate a theory. Copernicus' view that the sun was the centre of circular planetary motion made it difficult to calculate the location of Mars and Jupiter. The simple theory of circular motion had to disregard facts, and it was not until Kepler replaced the circular orbits with elipses that the Copernican theory satisfied our first criterion. On the other hand, the earth-centred theory had developed its complexity in an effort to cope with astronomical facts.

In some cases, then, simplicity, even though it does not explain everything, can justify a tentative explanation; at other times, the fact that an hypothesis cannot do justice to the facts is sufficient to reject it, no matter how simple it may be.

In other words, our two criteria cannot on their own establish an explanation as completely reliable. C.S. Peirce says that any particular set of facts may have an indefinite number of possible explanations; and of that indefinite set, there may be quite a few that satisfy our second criterion, of simplicity.

Because there is no certainty about any explanation, even when it does explain all the facts in a simple way, we should never assert one definitively. It is still subject to question. Rather than being a *thesis*, something proven, it is only an *hypothesis*, something supposed. Indeed, some people call this form of reasoning not "argument to explanation" but "hypothesis", because the conclusion is still uncertain.

The critical test of an hypothesis, or proposed explanation, comes when we try to apply it. Any good explanation should not only connect together the puzzling facts with which we started, but also anticipate other facts yet to be considered. From a proposed explanation, one should be able to make a prediction and then see whether the prediction comes to pass. So, for example, Sherlock Holmes entices his colleague, Dr. Watson, into the dark bedroom to wait for the arrival of the poisonous swamp adder. Only when he hears the hiss and, by the light of the candle, sees the snake retreat up the bell-pull does he know that his hypothesis has been confirmed.

In a similar way, Albert Einstein, puzzling about some curious results of experiments conducted by Michelson and Morley, developed the special theory of relativity, which hypothesized that light does not travel in a straight line. But his proposed explanation was confirmed only when the light of a star, known to be behind the sun, could be seen during a total eclipse.

Not all hypotheses can be so easily tested. Weber's theory that Luther's conception of calling or vocation made Protestantism into the seed-bed of capitalism does not offer predictions that can easily be investigated. The more facts about European and North American culture it can be shown to cover, the more adequate it is shown to be. But it is extremely difficult to take account of all social and cultural facts. And researchers are tempted to select for consideration those that most clearly conform to their expectations. In history and sociology, it is hard to keep separate the process of selecting the facts for observation and the predictions that follow from an hypothesis.

In addition, societies and cultures are highly complex, with many different networks of relations intersecting. So, the search for simplicity in explanatory hypotheses inevitably leads to dismissing a number of facts as insignificant — the result of interfering conditions. And making successful predictions becomes more difficult since, come what may, complications will frustrate their coming to pass.

Nonetheless, any proposed explanation should lead to some predictions about facts and documents not already considered. And it will become more likely to the extent that those predictions prove to be accurate. A prediction that fails calls into question the hypothesis, and may even prove it to be false. This appeal to prediction, and the readiness to surrender an hypothesis because the predictions are wrong, is the ultimate test of an argument to explanation. It alone can provide some solid evidence that the reasoning is reliable.

One does, however, need to consider the kinds of predictions that are involved. The closer the predictions are to the original set of features that posed the puzzle, the more likely they are to be successful; so they provide weaker support for the theory. When the predictions concern a quite different kind of thing, and they nonetheless prove to be successful, they strengthen the explanation.

Thus, if Weber were to base his argument on Germany, Holland and Switzerland, and then draw some inferences to England and Scotland, which were also influenced by Lutheran and Calvinist ideas, the connection between the original information and the test would be too close to be very strong. Were he, however, to find a similar kind of connection with a sense of calling in Zoroastrian thought, leading to a greater tendency to capitalism among the Parsees (who practise that religion) than among their neighbouring Hindus or Muslims, his thesis would be stronger.

The observation of the star during the eclipse offered strong support for Einstein's theory of relativity because it was far removed from the area of Michelson and Morley's experiments, while still confirming the prediction.

In other words, we once again apply a pattern of similarity and difference. The greater the differences in successful predictions, the more reliable the inference to explanation. The greater the similarity in unsuccessful predictions, the less likely is the reasoning adequate. Because predictions use a relation between some facts as an analogy for others, they can be assessed using the criteria of analogical reasoning.

Once they can show evidence of successful prediction, reasoners may justifiably move from their sub-conclusion, 'explanation E would combine F^1, F^2, F^3...F^n into a single integrated pattern,' to their final conclusion, 'E serves as an explanation for S.'

So our final representation of the pattern of this kind of reasoning looks like this:

Sub-premise 1: Situation S has facts F^1, F^2, F^3...F^n.
Sub-premise 2: Analogue A relates items I^1, I^2, I^3...I^n, and these are similar to the facts in S.
Sub-conclusion/Premise 1: So explanation E (which is what A would look like in situation S) would combine F^1, F^2, F^3...F^n into a single, integrated pattern.
Premise 2: On the basis of explanation E we have made predictions P^1, P^2, P^3...P^n and they have been successful.
Conclusion: So E serves as an explanation for S.

Because successful prediction is important in making the move from sub-conclusion to conclusion, it needs to be taken into account in our original assessment of the hypothesis. A good explanation is one that can in fact be easily tested using predictions.

One that would be true whatever happened does not take us very far. For example, some religious people believe that whatever happens is the will of God. Whenever good fortune dawns, the hypothesis is confirmed. If calamity occurs, that too establishes the explanation. But such a theory cannot really explain why things are the way they are; why they are not otherwise. For no matter what actually happens will be called God's will.

In a similar way some social theories are untestable. Committed capitalists will attribute all positive historical developments to free markets and a lack of government intervention. Events that on the surface do not support that thesis are made to fit by introducing sub-explanations and sub-hypotheses, or by appealing to complicating circumstances. Nothing is allowed that will disprove the theory. Once again we have an explanation that does not really explain.

In other words, a good explanation *should allow for some kind of testing that could in theory prove it false*. This then becomes our third criterion for assessing the sub-argument, even before we get to establishing our main conclusion.

An argument to an explanation takes as its first premise a set of puzzling facts. They may be more regular than one would normally expect, or they may offer an unexpected association of things. One looks for an analogy to serve as a second premise before concluding with a possible explanation that fits all the facts, is relatively simple, and can be tested. This hypothesis is then actually tested by making predictions and noting whether they are successful or not. Successful predictions warrant an inference to a final conclusion that the explanation is true of the original situation.

The sub-argument can be assessed by considering: first, whether the proposed explanation fits all the puzzling facts; second, whether it is "simple"— whether it appeals to networks of relations that are not artificially complicated; and third, whether the hypothesis allows testing by successful (or failed) predictions.

The final argument can be assessed by considering whether the predictions made concern things which are close to, or quite divergent from, the kinds of features already taken into account. The more divergent the successful predictions are, the more reliable the conclusion. On the other hand, where predictions fail, the closer they are to the original features, the more likely that the conclusion is wrong.

Sometimes investigators do not develop explanations in the framework of an argument. Instead of stating puzzling facts, proposing a hypothesis, and then looking for confirmation, they simply offer a description of history or nature that ties a number of facts together into an ordered pattern.

Thus, in *The Communist Manifesto*, Marx and Engels start by simply asserting their hypothesis that "the history of all hitherto existing society is the history of class struggles." Then they provide an account of the past that ties together a number of events and movements under this explanatory rubric:

> In the earlier epochs of history we find almost everywhere a complicated arrangement of society into various orders, a manifold of gradation of social rank. In ancient Rome we have patricians, knights, plebians and slaves; in the Middle Ages, feudal lords, vassals, guildmasters, journeymen, apprentices, serfs; in almost all of these classes, again, subordinate gradations.
> The modern bourgeois society that has sprouted from the ruins of feudal society has not done away with class antagonisms. It has but established new classes, new conditions of oppression, new forms of struggle in place of the old ones.

In a similar way, Rachel Carson's *Silent Spring* explains why "the voices of spring" have been silenced in America by setting out details of biochemical research, descriptions of natural catastrophes, and anecdotes of initiatives taken. These facts fit together into a comprehensible and "simple" whole once the widespread, but unnecessary, use of chemical insecticides and weed killers is offered as the explanation.

It is easy to miss the argument to explanation in such texts. In the first place, they do not always distinguish the puzzling facts from the hypothesis proposed. *The Com-*

munist Manifesto combines them into a single story. *Silent Spring* regularly uses the explanatory language of cause in giving its account of what has happened.

In the second place, they are not presented tentatively, as possibilities subject to further testing; they are asserted as definitely true. The obviousness of the fit is supposed to be enough to establish credibility. Note the dogmatic confidence of Marx and Engels' first sentence, quoted above.

Nonetheless, in both cases we have an argument to explanation, the proposal of an hypothesis.

While it has been relatively easy to make and test predictions when dealing with Carson's thesis about chemicals, it becomes more difficult to do so when we turn to explanations of history and society, like those of Marx and Weber, where we do not have the possibility of setting up controlled experiments. There, our method of assessment may have to stop with the questions of fit and simplicity. But that means that we can justify only the sub-conclusion of their argument. We have no way of establishing the final conclusion: that E *does* in fact explain S — that class struggle *does* explain all previous history.

One needs to be on guard, then, when one encounters confident explanations that hide their inferential character. Be careful to distinguish between the account of facts known and experienced, and the explanation or interpretation that is to provide a network or pattern of meaning. Those explanations and interpretations need to be assessed with care. Do they fit *all* the facts? Or has the researcher selected only those facts that do in fact conform, conveniently ignoring all the others? Are they really simple, in that the analogies they draw are relatively uncomplicated? Are there any ways by which we can easily test the likelihood of the hypothesis? Whenever the answer to the last question is *no*, we need to apply the other assessments especially carefully and well. Or else we may be led down the garden path.

EXERCISE:

For each of the following passages: (1) Identify (a) the facts that raised the initial question, asking for an explanation, as well as (b) the explanation that is proposed. (2) Assess the explanation in terms (a) of covering *all* the facts (including any you are aware of not explicitly mentioned), and (b) of being relatively simple. If appropriate, (3) suggest what kinds of predictions could be made to test the hypothesis. (4) List any alternative explanations that have been raised and rejected together with the criteria they do not satisfy.

> EXAMPLE: "Organs in a rudimentary condition plainly show that an early progenitor has the organ in a fully developed condition; and this in some cases implies an enormous amount of modification in the descendants. Throughout whole classes various structures are formed on the same pattern, and at a very early age the embryos closely resemble each other. Therefore I cannot doubt that the theory of descent with modification embraces all the members of the same great class or kingdom." C. Darwin, *The Origin of the Species.*

Facts to be explained: 1. Organs in a rudimentary condition; 2. throughout whole classes, various structures are formed on the same pattern and at a very early age the embryos closely resemble each other. (Notice that the phrases "plainly show that" and "this... implies" suggest moves towards a conclusion, and therefore the phrases "an early progenitor has the organs in a fully developed condition," and "an enormous amount of modification in the descendants" are parts of the explanation, not parts of the facts to be explained.)

Explanation: All the members of a single great class or kingdom have descended with considerable modification from an early progenitor. (Here we have taken the two phrases mentioned above, together with the "therefore" clause at the end, and reworked it into a statement of what the "theory of descent with modification" involves.)

   Assessment:

1. This explanation covers the facts mentioned. However, there is a lot of zoological data, and those of us who are not biologists are uncertain about how this explanation might handle other known facts.
2. The theory is simple and uncomplicated.
3. The theory can be tested by observing over time species placed in alien environments to see whether modifications do take place.

   No alternative hypotheses are mentioned.

1. That man is wearing a dark pin-stripe suit; he is carrying a briefcase; and he has an expression of knowing what he is doing. I conclude that he is probably a business man.

2. "This hat is three years old. These flat brims curled at the edge came in then. It is a hat of the very best quality. Look at the band of ribbed silk and the excellent lining. If this man could afford to buy so expensive a hat three years ago, and has had no hat since, then he has assuredly gone down in the world." A Conan Doyle, "The Adventure of the Blue Carbuncle"

3. Mary is not eating the way she used to; she daydreams a lot; and she becomes really interested whenever she hears Jack's name mentioned. I would guess she is in love.

4. The 747 disappeared suddenly from the radar screen; on the radio transmissions and voice recorders there were no indications that the pilots were aware of difficulties. Several 747 planes have been grounded because of structural problems and indeed two have had weak sections blown off by pressure differential. Although parallel shards of metal were found perforating luggage from the tail section, it must remain most likely that the 747 suffered from acute metal fatigue which caused the crash.

5. During a 1989 conference on the environment held in London, Prime Minister Margaret Thatcher advocated taking prompt action against the future use of chlorofluorocarbons. Some commentators said that Thatcher, who began her working career as a chemist, didn't want to seem indifferent to this kind of threat to mankind. But she probably made her decision on the same basis she has used in the past — how it would benefit her politically in the future. Thatcher, already elected three times in a row, wants to be the first British prime minister to govern four terms in succession. The next British national election is not due until 1991. It will take that long to begin reducing the world manufacture of chlorofluorocarbons.

6. "How can A and not-A, being and non-being, reality and negation, be thought together without mutual elimination and destruction? We need not expect anyone to answer the question other than as follows: They mutually *limit* one another." J.G. Fichte, *Third Fundamental Principle of the Entire Science of Knowledge.*

7. "Archimedes made many wonderful discoveries of different kinds, but of all these that which I shall now explain seems to exhibit a boundless ingenuity. When Hiero was greatly exalted in the royal power at Syracuse, in return for the success of his policy he determined to set up in a certain shrine a golden crown as a votive offering to the immortal gods. He let out the work for a stipulated payment, and weighed out the exact amount of gold for the contractor. At the appointed time the contractor brought his work skilfully executed for the king's approval, and he seemed to have fulfilled exactly the requirement about the weight of the crown. Later information was given that gold had been removed and an equal weight of silver added in the making of the crown. Hiero was indignant at this disrespect for himself, and, being unable to discover any means by which he might unmask the fraud, he asked Archimedes to give it his attention. While Archimedes was turning the problem over, he chanced to come to the place of bathing, and there, as he was sitting down in the tub, he noticed that the amount of water which flowed over the tub was equal to the amount by which his body was immersed. This indicated to him a means of solving the problem, and he did not delay, but in his joy leapt out of the tub and, rushing naked towards his home, he cried out with a loud voice that he had found what he sought. For as he ran he repeatedly shouted in Greek, *heureka, heureka*.

"Then, following up his discovery, he is said to have made two masses of the same weight as the crown, the one of gold and the other of silver. When he had so done, he filled a large vessel right up to the brim with water, into which he dropped the silver mass. The amount by which it was immersed in the vessel was the amount of water which overflowed. Taking out the mass, he poured back the amount by which the water had been depleted, measuring it with a pint pot, so that as before the water was made level with the brim. In this way he found what weight of silver answered to a certain measure of water.

"When he had made this test, in like manner he dropped the golden mass into the full vessel. Taking it out again, for the same reason he added a measured quantity of water, and found that the deficiency of water was not the same, but less; and the amount by which it was less corresponded with the excess of a mass of silver, having the same weight, over a mass of gold. After filling the vessel again, he then dropped the crown itself into the water, and found that more water overflowed in the case of the crown than in the case of the golden mass of identical weight; and so, from the fact that more water was needed to make up the deficiency in the case of the crown than in the case of the mass, he calculated and detected the mixture of silver with gold and the contractor's fraud stood revealed." Vitruvius, *On Architecture*.

8. "It has for some years been remarked that the remote spiral nebulae are, to all appearances, rushing away from the earth, and so presumably also from one another, at terrific speeds, which become greater and greater the farther they recede into space.... There is room for a good deal of doubt as to whether these huge speeds are real or not. They have not been obtained by any direct process of measurement, but are deduced by an application of what is known as Doppler's principle. It is a matter of common observation that the noise emitted by a motor-car horn sounds deeper in pitch when it is receding from us than when it is coming towards us. On the same principle the light emitted by a receding body appears redder in colour than that emitted by a body approaching us, colour in light corresponding to pitch in sound. By accurately measuring the colour of well-defined spectral lines, the astronomer is able to discover whether the body emitting them is approaching us or receding from us, and can estimate the speed of that motion. And the only reason for thinking that the distant nebulae are receding from us is that the light we receive from them appears redder than it ought normally to be." J. Jeans, *The Mysterious Universe*.

9. "After that I reflected upon the fact that I doubted, and that, in consequence, my spirit was not wholly perfect, for I saw clearly that it was a greater perfection to know than to doubt. I decided to ascertain from what source I had learned to think of something more perfect than myself, and it appeared evident that it must have been from some nature which was in fact more perfect. As for my ideas about many other things outside of me, as the sky, earth, light, heat, and thousands of other things, I was not so much troubled to discover where they came from, because I found nothing in them superior to my own nature. If they really existed, I could believe that whatever perfection they possessed might be derived from my own nature; if they did not exist, I could believe that they were derived from nothingness, that is, they were derived from my own defects. But this could not be the explanation of my idea of a being more perfect than my own. To derive it from nothingness was manifestly impossible, and it is no less repugnant to good sense to assume what is more perfect comes from and depends on the less perfect than it is to assume that something comes from nothing, so that I could not assume that it came from myself. Thus the only hypothesis left was that this idea was put in my mind by a nature that was more perfect than I was, which had all the perfections that I could imagine, and which was, in a word, God." R. Descartes, *Discourse on Method*.

10. An explanation for the Hindu prohibition against cattle slaughter:

"The practice arose to prevent the population from consuming the animal on which Indian agriculture depends. During the First Millenium B.C., the Ganges Valley became one of the most densely populated regions of the world.

"Where previously there had been only scattered villages, many towns and cities arose and peasants farmed every available acre of land. Kingsley Davis, a population expert at the University of California at Berkeley, estimates that by 300 B.C. between 50 million and 100 million people were living in India.

The forested Ganges valley became a windswept semidesert and signs of ecological collapse appeared; droughts and floods became commonplace, erosion took away the rich topsoil, farms shrank as population increased, and domesticated animals became harder and harder to maintain.

"It is probable that the elimination of meat eating came about in a slow, practical manner. The farmers who decided not to eat their cows, who saved them for procreation to produce oxen, were the ones who survived the natural disasters. Those who ate beef lost the tools with which to farm. Over a period of centuries, more and more farmers probably avoided beef until an unwritten taboo came into existence.

"Only later was the practice codified by the priesthood. While Indian peasants were probably aware of the role of cattle in their society, strong sanctions were necessary to protect zebus from a population faced with starvation. To remove temptation, the flesh of cattle became taboo and the cow became sacred." Marvin Harris, "India's Sacred Cow," *Human Nature*, 1978.

11. "'You see, Watson,' he explained in the early hours of the morning as we sat over a glass of whisky and soda in Baker Street, 'it was perfectly obvious from the first that the only possible object of this rather fantastic business of the advertisement of the League, and the copying of the Encyclopaedia, must be to get this not over-bright pawnbroker out of the way for a number of hours every day. It was a curious way of managing it, but, really, it would be difficult to suggest a better. The method was no doubt suggested to Clay's ingenious mind by the colour of his accomplice's hair. The four pounds a week was a lure which must draw him, and what was it to them, who were playing for thousands? They put in the advertisement, one rogue has the temporary office, the other rogue incites the man to apply for it, and together they manage to secure his absence every morning in the week. From the time that I heard of the

assistant having come for half wages, it was obvious to me that he had some strong motive for securing the situation.'

"'But how could you guess what the motive was?'

"'Had there been women in the house, I should have suspected a mere vulgar intrigue. That, however, was out of the question. The man's business was a small one, and there was nothing in his house which could account for such elaborate preparations, and such an expenditure as they were at. It must, then, be something out of the house. What could it be? I thought of the assistant's fondness for photography, and his trick of vanishing into the cellar. The cellar! There was the end of this tangled clue. Then I made enquiries as to this mysterious assistant and found that I had to deal with one of the coolest and most daring criminals in London. He was doing something in the cellar — something which took many hours a day for months on end. What could it be, once more? I could think of nothing save that he was running a tunnel to some other building.

"'So far I had got when we went to visit the scene of action. I surprised you by beating upon the pavement with my stick. I was ascertaining whether the cellar stretched out in front or behind. It was not in front. Then I rang the bell, and, as I hoped, the assistant answered it. We have had some skirmishes, but we had never set eyes upon each other before. I hardly looked at his face. His knees were what I wished to see. You must yourself have remarked how worn, wrinkled, and stained they were. They spoke of those hours of burrowing. The only remaining point was what they were burrowing for. I walked around the corner, saw the City and Suburban Bank abutted on our friend's premises, and felt that I had solved my problem. When you drove home after the concert I called upon Scotland Yard and upon the chairman of the bank directors, with the result that you have seen.'" A. Conan Doyle, "The Red-Headed League."

CHAPTER 8

REASONING FOR ACTION

In 1977, Mr. Justice Thomas R. Berger presented to the Canadian Minister of Indian Affairs and Northern Development the final report of his Inquiry into the Mackenzie Valley Pipeline proposed for the North. He summed up his report in these words:

A Mackenzie Valley pipeline should be postponed for ten years. If it were built now, it would bring limited economic benefits, its social impact would be devastating, and it would frustrate the goals of native land claims. Postponement would allow sufficient time for native claims to be settled, and for new programs and new institutions to be established. This does not mean that we must renounce our northern gas and oil. But it does mean that we must allow sufficient time for an orderly, not hasty, program of exploration to determine the full extent of our oil and gas reserves in the Mackenzie Delta and the Beaufort Sea. Postponement will offer time for you and your colleagues to make a rational determination regarding the priorities to be adopted in relation to the exploitation of all our frontier oil and gas resources, at a time when the full extent of our frontier reserves has been ascertained. [xxvii, Reproduced with permission of the Minister of Supply and Services Canada, 1989.]

Berger's task had been to make a recommendation to the government about actions it should take to prepare for the future. That recommendation, the first sentence in the excerpt quoted above, was stated as the conclusion of an argument. The rest of the passage provided reasons to support it. We could standardize the argument as follows:

Premise 1: Building the pipeline now would have limited economic benefit.
Premise 2: Building the pipeline now would have a devastating social impact.
Premise 3: Building the pipeline now would frustrate the goals of native land claims.
Premise 4: Postponement would allow sufficient time for native claims to be settled.
Premise 5: Postponement would allow time for new programs and institutions to be established.
Premise 6: We must allow sufficient time for an orderly program of exploration to determine the full extent of our oil and gas reserves.
Premise 7: Postponement will offer time for the minister and his colleagues to make a rational determination regarding the priorities to be adopted in relation to the exploitation of all our frontier oil and gas resources, at a time when the full extent of our frontier reserves has been ascertained.
Conclusion: A Mackenzie Valley pipeline should be postponed for ten years.

Each of the premises provides support for the conclusion. The first three argue against building the pipeline now; the last four argue for postponement. They are somewhat in parallel, since Premise 5 balances Premise 2, Premise 4 responds to Premise 3, and Premises 6 and 7 relate to the theme of Premise 1. Yet each one independently supports the recommendation Berger is making. They *converge* on the conclusion.

This kind of reasoning concludes with a suggestion about practice; it argues that something be done. In this case the commission has been asked to recommend policy to government. But similar considerations are involved whenever an institution or group of people get together to decide what to do in the future. When a business, for example, is deciding what kinds of products to develop, they have to find a course of action that will satisfy a number of premises. Individuals go through the same process of calculation in making decisions, whether about buying a new car or about resigning a secure position to take a new job.

The process of deciding what to do in practice takes place in the recesses of our innermost thoughts. But frequently as individuals, and inevitably as members of groups or institutions, we have to spell out the basis for our decisions in words, and at those points we open our reasoning to public assessment.

It is tempting at such times to plead a case — that is, to provide only reasons *for* doing a certain action or *against* alternatives. But this kind of argument is partial. Because it does not take into account any reasons for adopting other options or any problems its recommendation might have, it does not provide a complete picture.

In such reasoning the people developing the argument start out with a favourite course of action. They consider only the reasons that justify the conclusion they prefer and ignore everything that works against it. A bias prevents them from considering all the factors, so that their conclusion is not as likely to turn out the way they expect. Business people had argued for the pipeline because it would increase opportunities for investment, but they disregarded the damage it would create in the environment and in the native communities. Native people saw only the way it would disrupt their society and its traditions; they did not consider what would happen were the market for muskrat skins to disappear. In addition, the fundamental values of the two parties were quite incompatible, one placing all its trust on economic development, the other treasuring the intimate contact with the land and its inhabitants. Berger's task was to consider all sides, and to find a solution that would produce the best results overall.

Thus the risk of partiality makes reasoning for action the most difficult to assess, and the most difficult to do well.

In any reasoning for action there are two kinds of premises involved. These can be classified as *values* and *facts*. Berger on the one hand took into account several values: economic development, respect for the culture of native peoples, maintaining a viable natural environment. On the other hand he anticipated what in fact would happen were the pipeline to be built: its effect on the migration of caribou and the life of the native villages, the impact of the technology used in building the pipeline, economic costs and benefits.

Any decision involves *values*. One action is preferred to another because it is more desirable: it will have good results; it is something we want; it avoids problems. Values are of many sorts: respect for people and the environment; immediate satisfaction of our wants for food or pleasure; beauty and aesthetic delight; wealth and progress; honesty and integrity; power and influence; a happy community. All of these may be adopted as positive values. But there are negative values as well — ones we want to avoid: insecurity; distrust and hatred; pain and suffering; violent anarchy; inconvenience; sterile lakes and plains; demotion; death.

Negative values may emerge at two places in our arguments: to reject some alternatives by giving *negative reasons*, and as *counter-considerations* which work against the conclusion we advance. Notice that negative reasons are quite different from counter-considerations. A counter-consideration admits that *the recommended action* will have some undesirable effects but allows for the recommendation anyway, because its merits outweigh its disadvantages. A negative reason recommends an action because *other options* will create even greater problems. In a similar way, we use positive values not only to support our claim, but to indicate counter-considerations — good things we must give up because we have not chosen another course of action.

We espouse so many values, negative as well as positive, that we seldom, if ever, think of all of them together. We become aware of some when they are threatened or lacking. Most of the time they are taken for granted. This complicates our reasoning for action. The premises involving values to which we appeal are those that are on our minds — that demand immediate attention. And so we frequently do not ask how the various options would affect other values.

Arguments for action do not usually state the values in question. The person developing the position assumes that they are shared with the people to whom the argument is directed, so values frequently are not given explicitly. Values appear as premises only where there is some question about them; either they are not common to everyone, or alternative values are being used to support a contrary recommendation. In standardizing such arguments, then, it is useful to identify those values that we have assumed to be shared.

The second kind of premise in reasoning for action involves *facts*. These are not simply facts about the present or past. They include predictions about what will happen in the future. Each of the alternative actions we consider will have its consequences; it will interact with circumstances to produce new situations. We cannot control in detail how our actions will fit in with those circumstances, and thus what future facts will happen. That depends on causal patterns in the world around us. In other words, in our reasoning we have to anticipate events in the future which we can neither control absolutely nor predict accurately.

It is one thing to know about the present and past. We can observe and investigate. It is another thing to know about the future. We learn to predict events in the future through our experience of what has happened in the past. And if our own experience is limited, we can appeal to others whose experience is broader or more specialized. Over time, then, we develop a sense of regular patterns that recur in the world. By applying that sense to the situation in which our decision is to be made we can anticipate some of the results that will stem from our action.

So Berger anticipates that building the pipeline immediately would have a devastating social impact and frustrate the goals of native land claims. He knows that postponement would allow time for remedial action. However, he does not know whether, in the recommended ten-year waiting period, the land claims would be settled, new programs and institutions would be established, or the minister and his colleagues would rationally determine priorities. His experience does not justify claiming that these actions would in fact be done. His predictions in these areas are therefore more modest.

There are three kinds of predictions, two of which are illustrated in our selection from the Berger Commission report:

— The first are those we are confident will happen based on our experience. Berger uses these to reject some of the possible alternatives.

— Second are those that depend on the decisions and actions of other people. Since that will depend on their reasoning, it cannot be determined in advance. However, the more convincing the reasons given in making the recommendation, the more likely will those reasons influence that subsequent argument. It is to influence this second kind of prediction that Berger fills his report with facts and figures about both technology and native traditions.

— Third are consequences that cannot be anticipated at all. Circumstances may combine to create results that are completely unforeseen. Events far away in another continent may have their impact on the North several years down the road. So a full canvassing of likelihoods has to allow for events that could not have been expected, even by the most careful observer. Berger could not have known in 1977 that lobbying in Europe against the use of leg traps would, ten years later, seriously affect the economy of muskrat trappers in the Mackenzie Valley.

Any reasoning for action should involve these three kinds of prediction. On the basis of present and past facts, it will make some confident predictions about the future. Where future values will be achieved only by the action of other people, it will marshal facts and predictions not only to justify its own conclusion but also to influence their reasoning. And it will allow that unexpected events may turn everything upside down, and be prepared for that risk.

Thus the second kind of premise used when we reason for action provides facts from the present and past together with predictions of future likelihoods. By combining these factual predictions with our values, expressed and implicit, we reject some alternatives and choose others.

Consequences have both negative and positive values. In making a decision or recommendation, we have to weigh the various likelihoods and find a way of accomplishing as much good and as little evil as possible.

Because a good argument for action must fit the various premises together, it resembles an argument to explanation. Both have to integrate a variety into a single result. But whereas the argument to explanation wants to find a single framework of meaning (or value) that will make sense of a variety of *facts*, making a recommendation or decision looks for an action that will satisfy as many *values* as possible given the way the world is in fact.

It is this combination of values and facts that makes reasoning for action so difficult. In an explanation we have a number of facts that we already know to be true, and we only need to find one explanation that will do justice to all of them. But in a decision, our various values will be satisfied only if our predictions fit with the world as it actually will be, once our action is done. The awkward nature of existence makes it difficult to achieve all of our goals at once. So we cannot satisfy the native claims *and* allow immediate economic development *and* create programs and institutions for a viable community all at once; we must choose from among them. This is why the best reasoning to action will provide counter-considerations. The givens of experience prevent the full satisfaction of all our ideals, and the recommendation or decision we make involves the surrender of some. The statement of counter-considerations indicates that we have taken this negative impact of our action into account.

As a result, the same set of premises can justify several different conclusions depending on the way we order our priorities. As well, the number of possible premises is so large that we seldom, if ever, consider all of them.

Conclusions, then, can be reached by several different routes:

1. We already know what action we think should be done, and so we marshal only those predictions and values that support it and reject alternatives. We ignore counter-considerations because they might frustrate our purposes.

These were the kind of arguments made by the lobbyists before the Mackenzie Valley Pipeline Inquiry. The oil and pipeline companies, the associations of environmentalists and native people, all presented briefs that only supported their predominant interest.

2. Certain options have consequences with strong negative value. To avoid them, we adopt any other choice that is available. We pay little attention to counter-considerations and whatever positive reasons there are for our choice.

A decision of that sort resulted from the Berger Report. The Commission had spent a great deal of time considering the Mackenzie Valley Pipeline and documenting its disadvantages. Once it was decided not to proceed with it, however, the government authorized the Alaska Highway pipeline. There was no similar examination of its merits or weaknesses. The decision was taken simply because an alternative had been closed.

In a similar way, we frequently make decisions in our personal lives more to escape situations we do not like than to adopt solutions that have some prospect of success.

For example, early in his career Lester Pearson, later Prime Minister, thought he might become a lawyer.

I was duly articled, paid some fees, and began to study as instructed Anson's *Law of Contract*. This was the dullest book which I had ever read and I was told I would have to read many more like it. After four years away from books, followed by a four-month crash course of reading for my degree, the prospect of another two or three years of lectures, clerical work in a law office, and Anson on contracts became abhorrent. It occurred to me that I had no wish to become a man of law. [L.B. Pearson, *Mike*.]

It was negative reasons that led Pearson to leave his legal apprenticeship. There is no evidence that he had a positive goal he wanted to achieve.

3. We start with a limited number of options. We evaluate each one as carefully as we can, anticipating consequences and balancing values. At times it will be clear that one is better than the others, and the decision will be relatively easy. At times, however, some of the alternatives will turn out to be equally balanced (especially when the uncertainty of the future is taken into account). In this case the decision involves rating some values ahead of others. It thereby creates a scale of values.

When we go out to buy a house, we may look at half a dozen and then sit down to figure out which will serve our purposes the best: the one that is nearer good schools, the one that has more bedrooms, the one that is easier to finance, the one that is in a more attractive neighbourhood, and so on. We make our calculations as carefully as possible so that later we will be less likely to regret our choice.

This is similar to the task governments assign to Royal Commissions. Removed from the conflicts of politics, the commissioners have a chance to consider all the alternatives, evaluate their likely consequences, and outline the values that will be both honoured and ignored. Their recommendation is then taken into account in the political decision. (Although the politicians may then bring in other values that affect the final choice, such as regional disparities, ideological commitments, and the wish to be reelected.)

4. We create new alternatives. Faced with the recalcitrance of facts, we make a way that will satisfy more goals and desires than the choices with which we started. These are the most effective decisions and recommendations for they find some way of doing justice to almost all of our values, even those that originally appeared incompatible.

This is what Mr. Justice Berger attempted to do. His original choice was: Pipeline, yes or no. But he began to realize that there were other options: postponement; combining the building of the pipeline with a serious settlement of native claims and an innovative policy in social development. His investigation made him realize that the situation was much more complicated than it at first appeared. The recommendation he finally formulated met a number of conditions that all the original alternatives ignored.

Partial support for something we wanted to do in the first place; reaction against things we know we shall dislike; calculation of the pros and cons of a set of given alternatives; creating a course of action that had not previously been considered: these are four ways of moving from premises to conclusion.

There is, then, no neat way to evaluate reasoning for action. Each combination of goals and predictions allows an indefinite number of solutions. As a result no assessment can be final. Nonetheless, some decisions are certainly better than others: they satisfy more values; the agents are not as unpleasantly surprised by what in fact occurs. So there are several criteria for deciding when reasoning is strong and when weak.

In the first place, any action will have results that would otherwise not take place. As we have seen, we can anticipate some of these on the basis of our experience. And if our experience is limited we can get advice from people who *are* experienced. Therefore our decision will be better when our predictions cover more ground. Do we consider likely consequences we would not like as well as those we would? Do we admit that things may turn out differently from what we intend? Do we recognize that some of our desired goals depend on the decisions of other people?

This criterion is rather like the criterion of testability in reasoning to explanation. But there, when the tests fail we can go back to square one and formulate a new explanation. When deciding how to act, however, we are given no second chance. An action, once performed, cannot be called back. The train of consequences is set in motion.

A decision is good, then, when we are prepared to live with the results of what we do, and when it leads to no unexpected consequences that we should have been able to foresee.

In the second place, the conclusion should do justice to as many values as possible. It should be comprehensive, and consider positive as well as negative reasons. When we simply react against something we do not like we frequently land in situations that are worse. So we should be able to give reasons *for* our choice and not simply *against* alternatives.

Because it is usually not possible to satisfy all our desires, the negative implications of the conclusion need to be taken into account as well. Some goals will not be achieved, and may even be frustrated, by the decision taken. The more thoroughly such counter-considerations have been canvassed in making the decision, the more reliable will the final result be.

In reaching a decision through an argument to action, then, we should integrate as many values as possible. This reasoning will be the stronger, the more careful we are in calculating likely results—the more reliable our predictions.

In the third place, a simple conclusion will be better, because it will be that much easier to put into practice. The more complications there are, and the more people that have to be involved, the more likely it is that the final action will not turn out to be quite what was envisaged. The very fact that Berger's recommendation involved creative government policy in establishing programs and institutions and in settling native claims made it less likely that it would be implemented in just the way he had imagined.

The three criteria for assessment, then, are
— how thoroughly have likely consequences been considered?
— how many positive values will be enhanced and how many negative values avoided?
— how simple will it be to bring the action about?

These three considerations tend to work against each other. For simple decisions frequently ignore complicating factors; and recommendations that try to satisfy too many values are not easy to implement. But the best kind of reasoning to action satisfies all of these requirements at once. That is frequently a tall order. That is why creativity is frequently needed.

A person with a good deal of experience, and who has learned from history, will have a better sense of the kinds of contingencies that could crop up, and of the success of different sorts of actions. He or she has, if you will, a wider range of analogues to choose from when considering how the various premises can be combined into a single recommendation or decision. For no two situations are alike. The variety of facts and diversity of values makes decision difficult. Yet with all the differences in circumstances, those who are wise can spot similarities. And they sense how the similarities will be affected by the differences. The experience that produces good arguments for action is nothing but developing skill in analogical reasoning.

Reasoning to action has as its conclusion a decision or a policy recommendation. Its premises are made up of a number of values — goals and desires both positive and negative — as well as predictions about the future based on things present or past. Since few decisions can satisfy all goals, there will usually be counter-considerations to balance some of the positive premises.

To assess an argument of this sort, three things need to be taken into account: 1. how much have the factual conditions that will affect success been taken into account? 2. how far does the decision or recommendation satisfy all of the goals in question? and 3. how simple and easily executed is the decision or recommendation?

There may be a number of possible conclusions that appear equally satisfactory. In making a decision the agent must be ready to accept the negative consequences that will result, either intentionally or unintentionally, from his or her action. To excuse ourselves because we did not know indicates that the initial reasoning was not carefully done.

EXERCISE:

Standardize the following arguments leading to policy recommendations or decisions. Indicate reasons for rejecting alternatives (negative reasons), counter-considerations and positive support. If appropriate, identify values that are assumed. Assess the reasoning for action using the three criteria of anticipating consequences, realizing values, and simplicity.

EXAMPLE: "The breakdown of the family irrespective of cause creates an identity problem for its members and their role may become irreversibly distorted. Their circumstances are such that their problems are frequently perpetuated from generation to generation. Economic poverty is an additional burden to the unnatural circumstances which exist. The single parent who is left with adequate financial support has a far greater opportunity to maintain a stable family unit than one who must depend on public support....

"Day-care service for the pre-school child is a luxury for some, a strong emotional support for others and a financial impossibility for many who need this kind of care. Such a service may free the mother to return to the labour force, become more fulfilled as a person and thus become a more adequate parent to her child. We recommend such services should be recognized in all areas of our country as worthy of tax support, making it possible for voluntary groups, already active in this field, to meet the growing need." "Brief to the Special Senate Committee on Poverty," The Salvation Army, Canada, Commission on Moral and Social Standards and Issues, 1970.

Standard form:

P1. The breakdown of the family creates an identity problem for its members.
P2. These problems are frequently perpetuated from generation to generation.
P3. Economic poverty complicates the situation.

P4. The single parent with adequate financial support can more easily maintain a stable family unit. (So it is better to have a working single parent than one who is confined at home looking after children with an inadequate income.)

P5. A day care service may free the mother to return to the labour force, become more fulfilled as a person, and thus become a more adequate parent to her child.

(All of these five premises are linked together in providing support for the conclusion.)

P6. Day care service is a luxury for some and a financial impossibility for many who need this kind of care.

(This premise supports the claim that day care should be tax supported.)

P7. Day care service is a strong emotional support for some people.

C. Day care services, even by voluntary groups, should be recognized as worthy of tax support.

All the premises provide positive support for the conclusion.

Implicit values: Childhood identity problems are bad. Emotional security and personal fulfilment are good. Stable family units are based on adequate parents.

Assessment:

1. This document makes claims about family breakdown, personality problems and poverty and their connections. It does not cover any facts about the need for additional people in the work force, nor about the tax cost of day care versus the tax received from extra employment (and the amount otherwise payed in welfare and mothers' allowances).

2. The argument adopts values of personal fulfillment and self-respect. It does not refer to economic values or values of individual responsibility.

3. The recommendation is simple to implement, although tax support will require some regulations and supervision to ensure the proper use of funds.

1. You should return books to the library on time. When borrowing them, you in effect contract to do so. Also, other people may need them, and you can avoid expensive fines.

2. We recommend that the government abolish differential fees for foreign students. While this will mean that they will be getting benefits for which they or their parents have not paid taxes, it will nevertheless make a contribution to international understanding as these students will take back their memories of Canada when they go home. It will also benefit Canadian students because they will have contact with a wider world. In addition, many of the foreign students come from countries which have a much lower standard of living than Canada, and cannot afford the exhorbitant fees that are being charged.

3. Because all 14 of the academic administrative posts [in the university] are currently held by men, the lack of senior women in the non-academic management sector is especially discouraging. At this time, there are four women in the top twenty Staff Association positions, and four (of 29) in the senior non-academic administrative group who are excluded from the Staff Association. With only two men at the Director level due to retire within the next four years, it is unlikely that this situation can change significantly in the immediate future. However, about one-third of the male support staff (including four of the senior non-academic administrators) are now between fifty and sixty-

five years of age, so this group will begin retiring in greater numbers in the mid 1990's. It seems sensible for the university to capitalize on its human resource potential by starting now to train support staff, including women, to move into positions of responsibility when they become available. [Note that the Staff Association, the Directors, and support staff all refer to non-academic positions.]

4. Everyone should visit Paris in 1989. Since it is the bicentennial of the French Revolution, there are lots of extra events being planned. The French government has now dropped its requirement that Canadians have visas to enter the country. And Paris is one of the most splendid cities of the world, with its parks, shops, museums and historic buildings.

5. "In sum, then, I suggest that complete sex is superior to less complete sex because it is conducive to psychological well-being, involves a particular kind of respect for persons, and is frequently coincident with valued emotions which are productive of virtue." Sara Ruddick, "On Sexual Morality"

6. "Thus it is clear that the main tenet of Socialism, the community of goods, must be utterly rejected; for it would injure those whom it is intended to benefit, it would be contrary to the natural rights of mankind, and it would introduce confusion and disorder into the commonwealth. Our first and most fundamental principle, therefore, when we undertake to alleviate the condition of the masses, must be the inviolability of private property." Pope Leo XIII, *Rerum Novarum*.

7. "I was homesick only for a few months, but soon it became clear that I had no wish to remain in business,

however, successful I might become; nor did I want to live in Chicago or indeed in any part of the United States for the rest of my life. In short, I wanted to remain a Canadian in Canada, to finish my education, for I now realized I had not done so in spite of my degree, and then teach history or political science at a university. During the winter of 1921, I knew, for the first time, what I really wanted to do with the years ahead." L.B. Pearson, *Mike*.

8. Simone de Beauvoir refers to a debate in John Dos Passos's *The Adventures of a Young Man*. "Following a strike, some American miners are condemned to death. Their comrades try to have their trial reconsidered. Two methods are put forward: one can act officially, and one knows that they then have an excellent chance of winning their case; one can also work up a sensational trial with the Communist Party taking the affair in hand, stirring up a press campaign and circulating international petitions; but the court will be unwilling to yield to this intimidation. The party will thereby get a tremendous amount of publicity, but the miners will be condemned. What is a man of good will to decide in this case?

"Dos Passos's hero chooses to save the miners and we believe that he did right. Certainly, if it were necessary to choose between the whole revolution and the lives of two or three men, no revolutionary would hesitate; but it was merely a matter of helping along the party propaganda, or better, of increasing somewhat its chances of developing within the United States; the immediate interest of the Communist Party in that country is only hypothetically tied up with that of the revolution; in fact, a cataclysm like the war has so upset the situation of the world that a great part of the gains and losses of the past have been absolutely swept away. If it is really *men* which the movement claims to be serving, in this case it must prefer saving the lives of three concrete individuals to a very uncertain and weak chance of serving a little more effectively by their sacrifice the mankind to come." *The Ethics of Ambiguity*.

9. "The attachment which men feel to a right, and the respect which they display for it, is generally proportioned to its importance, or to the length of time during which they have enjoyed it. The rights of private persons among democratic nations are commonly of small importance, of recent growth, and extremely precarious — the consequence is that they are often sacrificed without regret, and almost always violated without remorse. But it happens that at the same period and among the same nations in which men conceive a natural contempt for the rights of private persons, the rights of society at large are naturally extended and consolidated: in other words, men become less attached to private rights at the very time at which it would be most necessary to retain and to defend what little remains of them. It is therefore most especially in the present democratic ages, that the true friends of liberty and the greatness of man ought constantly to be on the alert to prevent the power of government from lightly sacrificing the private rights of individuals to the general execution of its designs." A. de Tocqueville, *Democracy in America*.

10. "We have now recognized the necessity to the mental well-being of mankind (on which all their other well-being depends) of freedom of opinion, and freedom of the expression of opinion, on four distinct grounds, which we will now briefly recapitulate.

"First, if any opinion is compelled to silence, that opinion may, for aught we can certainly know, be true. To deny this is to assume our own infallibility.

"Secondly, though the silenced opinion be an error, it may, and very commonly does, contain a portion of truth;

and since the general or prevailing opinion on any subject is rarely or never the whole truth, it is only by the collision of adverse opinions that the remainder of the truth has any chance of being supplied.

"Thirdly, even if the received opinion be not only true, but the whole truth; unless it is suffered to be, and actually is, vigorously and earnestly contested, it will, by most of those who receive it, be held in the manner of prejudice, with little comprehension or feeling of its rational grounds. And not only this, but, fourthly, the meaning of the doctrine itself will be in danger of being lost or enfeebled, and deprived of its vital effect on the character and conduct: the dogma becoming a mere formal profession, inefficacious for good, but cumbering the ground and preventing the growth of any real and heartfelt conviction from reason or personal experience." J.S. Mill, *On Liberty*.

11. "Dear Mr. Smith:-

"After serious consideration I have decided that I should resign from the ministry of the Methodist Church. It is perhaps due both to the Conference and myself that I state, at least in outline, the considerations that have led me to this action.

"Within a short time after my ordination I was much troubled because my beliefs were not those that were commonly held and preached. The implications of the newer theological training which I received during my B.D. course and at Oxford revealed themselves with growing clearness and carried me far from the old orthodox position....

"As years went by, certain disquieting conclusions gradually took form. I began to see that the organized church had become a great institution with institutional aims and ambitions. With the existence of a number of denominations, this meant a keen rivalry. In many cases the interests of the community were made subservient to the interests of the church. Further, the church, as many other institutions, was becoming increasingly commercialized. This meant control of the policies of the church by men of wealth, and in many cases, the temptation of the minister to become a financial agent rather than a moral and spiritual leader. It meant also that anything like a radical programme of social reform became in practice almost impossible. In my own particular work amongst the immigrant peoples I felt that I, at least, could give more effective service outside denominational lines. Intellectual freedom was not enough – I must be free to work....

"In the meantime another factor makes my position increasingly difficult. The war has gone on now for four years.... For me, the teachings and spirit of Jesus are absolutely irreconcilable with the advocacy of war. Christianity may be an impossible idealism, but so long as I hold to it, ever so unworthily, I must refuse, as far as may be, to participate in or to influence others to participate in war....

"Holding the convictions that I do, what is my duty under such circumstances? The Christian Guardian [the Methodist magazine], presumably voicing the thought of the church, discusses the case in its issue of May 1st: '... In time of war the State has something at stake, and it rightly refuses to allow a peace propaganda to be carried on in its midst. Not only so but the church has a duty in the matter and that is to prevent unpatriotic speeches in her pulpits. And if the minister who is a confirmed pacifist has a right to speak his mind freely, the church which he serves reserves the right to see that he does not use her pulpits nor her authority to damage or defeat the efforts of patriots who are trying to win a righteous war. In every such case the country and the church have a right to insist not only on the absence of seditious or disloyal speech and action, but also on truest patriotic utterances, and if a man cannot conscientiously declare himself a patriot he has no business in any church which prides itself upon its patriotism.'

"Apparently the church feels that I do not belong and reluctantly I have been forced to the same conclusion. This decision means a crisis in my life. My associations, my education, my friends, my work, my ambitions have all been connected with the church. After twenty-two years it is hard to get out, not knowing whither I go. In taking this step, I have no sense of disloyalty to my honoured father or the upbringing of my widowed mother. On the other hand I have a growing sense of fellowship with the 'Master' and the goodly company of those who, throughout the ages, have endeavoured to 'follow the gleam.' I still feel the call of service and trust that I may have some share in the work of bringing in the Kingdom." Letter of J.S. Woodsworth, June 8, 1918.

12. "Thousands of years ago, the Egyptians believed that no soul could justify itself after death unless it could say, 'I have never let any one suffer from hunger.' All Christians know they are liable to hear Christ Himself say to them one day, 'I was an hungered, and ye gave me no meat.' Every one looks on progress as being, in the first place, a transition to a state of human society in which people will not suffer from hunger. To no matter whom the question may be put in general terms, nobody is of the opinion that any man is innocent if, possessing food for himself in abundance and finding someone on his doorstep three parts dead from hunger, he brushes past without giving him anything. So it is an eternal obligation toward the human being not to let him suffer from hunger when one has the chance of coming to his assistance." Simone Weil, *The Need for Roots*.

CHAPTER 9

IRREGULAR ARGUMENTS

When we scan the great literature of our tradition, we find a great many inferences that do not fit any of the patterns discussed so far. Nor do they fall into the much tighter category of deductive syllogisms, where a conclusion follows its premises simply because of their form. Nonetheless these arguments have played a significant rôle in developing our culture.

Because as a group they follow no pattern, it is not easy to categorize or evaluate them. Nonetheless, any discussion of non-deductive reasoning needs to consider them — and suggest a procedure for their assessment. The rules to follow will be general, rather than specific. And they will be applied in different ways to different arguments. With this in mind, we shall in this chapter simply provide several examples, indicating the kind of analysis and assessment that is appropriate. Each argument will be different from the others. And we must learn to concentrate on its particular content and form.

Let us start with a simple argument adapted from Aristotle:

Pleasure seems to be complete at any given moment; for it is a whole, and at no time can one find a pleasure whose form will be completed if the pleasure lasts longer. [*Nicomachean Ethics.*]

Our first step is to standardise the argument. We set it out with the premises first and the conclusion at the end:

Premise 1: Pleasure is a whole.
Premise 2: At no time can one find a pleasure whose form will be completed if the pleasure lasts longer.
Conclusion: Pleasure seems to be complete at any given moment.

As in any argument, the conclusion can be no more certain than the premises; and if the premises are false, they have no power to prove the conclusion true. For this reason, it makes sense to assess the premises first to decide whether there are good reasons for believing them to be true, or not — for accepting or rejecting them. If they are to be found wanting, the argument can be set aside.

In this case, we may have difficulty deciding how reliable the premises are, for we need to think carefully about our pleasures, and about whether they in fact are wholes, and whether duration can add to their completeness.

Once we have reached a decision about the reliability of the premises, we can begin to assess the strength of the support they provide for the conclusion.

The conclusion mentions several ideas: pleasure, being complete, and a given moment. But it connects them in a specific way: pleasure is positively characterized as complete (or at least appears to be so); that is, Aristotle is not *opposing* pleasure to completeness. And the positive connection applies at any particular moment; that is, it does not require *duration*. As in this example, we frequently clarify the nature of the connection asserted in the conclusion by identifying the contrasting claim that is being excluded.

In assessing the argument, we start from the conclusion, and the connection asserted in it. For the premises are to justify or establish that connection. And they do so by providing some bridging ideas—some intermediate terms that are more obviously connected with one or other of the ideas in the conclusion. Therefore we have two questions to ask: what are the intermediate terms provided by the premises? and how well do they strengthen the connection asserted in the conclusion?

In the first premise, pleasure is called a whole; the second asserts that a longer duration never serves to add to, or supplement, the form of pleasure. Our task is to consider how these two statements, either independently or together, bridge the connection between pleasure, completeness, and any given moment. The second premise rules out any rôle for duration; it supports the connection between completeness and any particular instant; however, it does not assert that completeness is present. That positive claim is provided by the first premise. The two seem to be connected through the terms: "whole" and "form". At first those words seem to be unrelated; but when we think through their meanings we may begin to realize that the form presents pleasure as a whole, and the whole, being intact, is expressed in the form. The two ideas are close relatives.

We noticed that relationship through reflection; we had to think carefully about what the words mean and how they fit into their context to see how the connection is made. It is this need to understand just what is being said that makes the assessment of many arguments so difficult. For frequently meanings are vague or obscure. Yet only when we have meanings clear can we begin to decide whether the premises provide strong support for the conclusion or not.

Now we are in a position to evaluate Aristotle's argument. If we take his premises at least for the sake of argument, do they provide adequate support for the conclusion he wants to maintain? They probably do. For Aristotle has not made an outright claim that pleasure *is* complete, but only that it *seems to be*. He is talking about appearance and probability, not about reality and certainty. The premises provide some evidence for the weaker claim that he makes, even if they would not support the stronger claim that he avoids.

With that we have completed our assessment of Aristotle's argument. Because at crucial points we were left with thinking through the meaning of what he said, we were not able to provide any neat rules for deciding whether the reasoning was strong or weak. We had to rely on our own, informed, judgement. Nonetheless, there was a pattern to what we did. We took three key steps:

— *First standardize;*
— *then consider whether you can accept the premises as reliable or not;*
— *finally identify the terms and connections in the conclusion and see whether the premises provide support for that particular connection.*

While these rules set out the procedure we should follow, they do not spell out what we should look for in making our assessment. For that we need practice.

Not all arguments are as simple or as straightforward as Aristotle's about pleasure. Sometimes they become quite complicated. Consider the following argument from Rousseau's *The Social Contract*:

The general will alone can direct the forces of the State according to the object of its institution, which is the common good; for if the opposition of private interests has rendered necessary the establishment of societies, the agreement of these same interests has rendered it possible. That which is common to these different interests forms the social bond; and unless there were some point in which all interests agree, no society could exist. Now, it is solely with regard to this common interest that the society should be governed.

We first standardize the argument by setting out the premises and the conclusion in order. The conjunction "for" in the middle of the first sentence suggests that the conclusion has just been given, and the premises are to follow. Once we set out the text in that way, we find that we have a set of reasons for a claim:

Premise 1: If the opposition of private interests has rendered necessary the establishment of societies, the agreement of these same interests has rendered it possible.
Premise 2: That which is common to these different interests forms the social bond.
Premise 3: Unless there were some point in which all interests agree, no society could exist.
Premise 4: It is solely with regard to this common interest that the society should be governed.
Conclusion: The general will alone can direct the forces of the State according to the object of its institution, which is the common good.

It is tempting to move immediately into the process of evaluating the premises and assessing the reasoning. But a few moments reflection suggests that something is wrong. For premises 1 and 3 are conditional statements, connecting two clauses, but not asserting anything definite. Yet it would seem that Rousseau needs to make categorical statements: "The agreement of private interests makes the establishment of societies possible." And "there is some point where all interests agree." We therefore need to modify the argument before we have our standardizing complete.

The common forms of deductive reasoning are so familiar and so obvious that they are frequently assumed in an argument through a kind of shorthand. One premise may be given; a second premise is assumed as generally known, so it is not stated. Together the two premises (the stated and the unstated) support a sub-conclusion. It is left to the readers to supply the unstated premise and draw the sub-conclusion themselves.

Consider Premise 3. "Unless...", as we know, is the logical equivalent of "If... not...". Therefore we can rewrite Premise 3: "If there were not some point in which all interests agree, no society could exist." However, we all know that societies do exist. So we have a form of *modus tollens*, or denying the consequent. Since societies *do* exist, we can conclude that there *is* some point in which all interests agree. This sub-conclusion now takes the place of the earlier Premise 3.

A similar result follows from Premise 1. If we had been reading through Rousseau's *The Social Contract*, we would know that Rousseau maintains that the opposition of private interests *has* rendered necessary the establishment of societies. Because he has affirmed the antecedent of the hypothetical statement in Premise 1, he has a *modus ponens*, from which we can conclude the consequent of the hypothetical statement: that the agreement of private interests has rendered possible the establishment of societies.

Even without that background information, we get a sense from the way Rousseau develops his paragraph that he is here interested in establishing the claim that private interests agree. He does not want to leave it questionable, as part of a complex, hypothetical statement. He appears to assume the truth of the antecedent, and hence the truth of the consequent as well.

Once we build in those two sub-arguments we have a more complicated standard form:

> **1P1**: If the opposition of private interests has rendered necessary the establishment of societies, the agreement of these same interests has rendered it possible. [Stated in our passage.]
> **1P2**: The opposition of private interests has rendered necessary the establishment of societies. [Established earlier in Rousseau's text.]
> **Premise 1**: The agreement of private interests has made it possible to establish societies. [Sub-conclusion.]
> **Premise 2**: That which is common to these different interests forms the social bond.
> **3P1**: Unless there were some point in which all interests agree, no society could exist. [Stated in our passage.]
> **3P2**: Societies do exist. [Common knowledge.]
> **Premise 3**: There is some point in which all interests agree. [Sub-conclusion.]
> **Premise 4**: It is solely with regard to this common interest that the society should be governed.
> **Conclusion**: So the general will alone can direct the forces of the State according to the object of its institution, which is the common good.

This, then, is the structure of the argument Rousseau puts forward, and we are now ready to assess the strength of its reasoning.

Before we begin considering whether the premises provide strong support for the conclusion, we need to consider the reliability of the premises. Are there good reasons for believing them to be true? Are there good reasons for rejecting them? Or do we just not have enough information to decide?

In this case, we can see that premises 2 and 4 will have to be assessed as simple statements. But when we turn to our new premises 1 and 3 the situation is more complicated. For each of them is the conclusion of a sub-argument. Since we constructed those sub-arguments to be deductively valid — *modus ponens* in the one case, and *modus tollens* in the other —, we can evaluate their reliability by considering whether their respective sub-premises are reliable. However, if those premises turn out to be weak, the sub-conclusion may still be true. (A bad argument does not *prove* its conclusion true; but it does not say it is false either. It could be true on other grounds.) Therefore we may still have to look at the sub-conclusions as independent statements.

We leave that assessment of acceptability up to you, the reader.

For our concern is with the third step in the process: Do the four premises offer strong evidence for the conclusion? We set them out again:

Premise 1: The agreement of private interests has made it possible to establish societies.
Premise 2: That which is common to these different interests forms the social bond.
Premise 3: There is some point in which all interests agree.
Premise 4: It is solely with regard to this common interest that the society should be governed.
Conclusion: So the general will alone can direct the forces of the State according to the object of its institution, which is the common good.

How do the premises support the conclusion? The conclusion contains several ideas: the general will, the forces of the state, and the common good as the object (or purpose) of the institutional state. It connects these ideas in a certain way: the common good is the standard for the way the forces of the state should be directed; and the general will is the only means available for maintaining that standard.

Neither phrase, "the general will" or "the state", appears in the premises. But we do have phrases like "the agreement of private interests", "that which is common to the different interests", "a point in which all interests agree," and "common interest". Because we tend to associate our *interests* with the kinds of things we *will*, and that which is *common* is also said to be *general*, we infer that Rousseau is trying to establish something called the general will by referring to common, or agreed-upon, interests. He assumes a connection in meaning between the phrases in the premises and the phrase in the conclusion.

There is a similar connection in meaning between "society" and "social bond" in the premises and the "State" of the conclusion. Even though the word "state" suggests an organized government (which the word "society" does not), it is always societies that are organized into states.

But the reasoning does not rely simply on that double shift of meaning or vocabulary. It also involves the relation between those terms. For the conclusion says that the general will should *direct* the state *to achieve its object or goal* (which, Rousseau says, is the common good). What is in the premises that can support that connection?

Once again we have to think through the meanings of terms. This involves three stages. First, what interests people is what they call good. And what interests all the people could then be considered the common good.

Secondly, what they share creates a social bond; it is the necessary condition for any society. And therefore (by incorporating the shift from society to state) we can conclude that their shared interests provide a central ingredient that allows a state to function. Thirdly, as we have already suggested, interests motivate people to act—they direct the will. So common interests (which, as we have seen, can shift in meaning to the general will) should direct the state.

These three sets of implications combine with the two shifts of meaning we noted earlier to lead Rousseau from his premises to his conclusion. They provide the intermediate stages that enable us to combine "general will", "the state", and "common good" in the way he wants to do.

This all seems very complicated. And one would like to have an easier, cut-and-dried way of tackling the argument. Unfortunately life and language are not that simple. Meanings are flexible and fluid. Some are conventions that have become enshrined in common usage; others depend on the varied experiences of those people who are speaking and writing; still others grow or atrophy over time, from one century to the next. In every case an argument that relies on meaning depends for its effectiveness on the background and capacity of those assessing it. Because of this variation, it is important to follow carefully the prescribed steps, and practice to make sure that every aspect of the argument has been considered.

Notice that it is not sufficient simply to have the same terms in the premises and the conclusion. Finding that "general will" is like "agreed common interests" and "State" is like "society and social bonds" is not enough. We need to go further to see if the way in which those terms are combined in the conclusion—the fact that the general will *should direct* the state—also has some support in the premises.

Once we have identified the elements in the premises that do support the conclusion, we are ready to assess the argument. For this there are no general rules. We are thrown on our own resources. We must think through what is meant by the premises, and what is meant by the conclusion. And we have to decide for ourselves whether it "makes sense": whether there really is support, or only some confusion of meaning.

At times it will not be hard. To give an extreme example, if we had as a premise "Man is fickle", and as conclusion "all humans are unreliable", we would soon spot the ambiguity in the two uses of the word "man". The argument moves from using it for male humans in the premise to using it as a generic term for all humans in the conclusion. We would soon reject such an argument as fallacious. But in the passage from Rousseau it is not so obvious that "society" and "state" are significantly different; and we may have to think for a while before we can decide that "common interests" is a synonym for "general will".

Sometimes it will be easy to see that an argument is a good one. By recognizing that two expressions *are* virtually synonyms — that they really mean the same thing — we can convert the passage into a syllogism.

As an example, we take the second and third premise in our selection from Rousseau:

Premise 2: That which is common to these different interests forms the social bond.
Premise 3: There is some point in which all interests agree.

On reflection we notice that "that which is common to the different interests" is rather like "the point in which all interests agree." So we could reorganize the two into a syllogism:

— That which is common to the different interests is what forms the social bond.
— Some point is that which is common to the different interests.

And we could draw from them the valid conclusion: "Some point is what forms the social bond." Or in more colloquial language, "There is something that forms the social bond."

In this case, by thinking about the terms and the relations we have been able to take two dissimilar statements and make them into a valid categorical argument.

But while some arguments will obviously have a fallacy (like the two meanings in the argument about "men"), and others will clearly be strong — even deductively valid, there will be many where it is much harder to decide. The greater sense we have for the conventional meaning of terms, or for the particular meanings intended by the author, the less difficult it will be. And the more experience we have in thinking through arguments the more expert we become.

Just as you cannot run the marathon without a lot of practice, so you cannot really master the skill of assessing arguments without doing it. But just as you learn to run well by listening to coaches and other experienced runners, so you will learn to reason well, not just by thinking on your own, but also by discussing your assessments with other people and learning from trained thinkers.

Our particular analysis of Rousseau's argument is not the only possible one, nor indeed the only correct one. We have tried to make as much sense out of what Rousseau has written as we can. But there may be things we have missed. So you should think through the argument yourself and make your own assessment.

In discussing the passage from Rousseau we followed the procedures suggested above at the end of our discussion of Aristotle's argument. We first standardized the argument. We asked whether we should accept the premises as true (even though we did not try to answer that question here). And we spelled out what it is in the premises that provides support for the conclusion. Thus, even though many arguments do not fit the standard forms we have discussed earlier, there is a procedure we can follow to help us make an informed assessment.

EXERCISE:

For each of the following passages, first, standardize the argument, second, consider whether the premises are reliable, third, analyse the conclusion and show how the premises provide support for the connection of terms asserted there. After reflection, indicate whether you think the argument is strong or weak, and give your reasons for that judgement.

EXAMPLE: "When the inhabitant of a democratic country compares himself individually with all those about him, he feels with pride that he is the equal of any one of them; but when he comes to survey the totality of his fellows, and to place himself in contrast to so huge a body, he is instantly overwhelmed by the sense of his own insignificance and weakness. The same equality which renders him independent of each of his fellow citizens taken separately, exposes him alone and unprotected to the influence of the greater number. The public has therefore among a democratic people a singular power, of which aristocratic nations could never so much as conceive an idea; for it does not persuade to certain opinions, but it enforces them, and infuses them into the faculties by a sort of enormous pressure of the minds of all upon the reason of each." A. de Tocqueville, *Democracy in America*.

Standardization: The "therefore" in the third sentence, and the "for" that comes after its semi-colon provide us with useful clues concerning the conclusion and the premise. And the "but" in the first sentence suggests a contrast or opposition, indicating that it is preceded by a counter-consideration. The result is:

Counter-consideration: When the inhabitant of a democratic country compares himself individually with all those about him, he feels with pride that he is the equal of any one of them.

Premise 1: When he comes to survey the totality of his fellows, and to place himself in contrast to so huge a body, he is instantly overwhelmed by the sense of his own insignificance and weakness.

Premise 2: The same equality which renders him independent of each of his fellow citizens taken separately, exposes him alone and unprotected to the influence of the greater number.

Premise 3: The public does not persuade to certain opinions, but it enforces them, and infuses them into the faculties by a sort of enormous pressure of the minds of all upon the reason of each.

Conclusion: The public has among a democratic people a singular power, of which aristocratic nations could never so much as conceive an idea.

Reliability: If these statements are taken as universal claims, applying to anyone whosoever, they are easily shown to be false. It is more likely, however, that de Tocqueville intends them as generalizations, applying to most, but not necessarily all people in democratic countries. In that event they appear plausible, and provide a reliable base for reasoning. Nonetheless, it is not easy to determine whether they are really true.

Analysis: The conclusion says that the public exerts "a singular power", or in other words, a strong influence, on a democratic people. And it contrasts this influence with the kinds of control known in countries with aristocratic governments. In this passage there is no other reference to aristocracies (although de Tocqueville has talked about them earlier), so we can leave that comparison aside for our present purposes.

The question, then, is: do the premises support the claim that the public exerts a strong influence in a democracy?

Well, the same terms are found in the premises. The pronoun "he" in premise 1 refers back to, and stands for, "the inhabitant of a democratic country," found in the counter-consideration. "The public" is expressly mentioned in Premise 3, and referred to elsewhere as "the totality of his fellows", "the greater number of his fellow citizens" and "the minds of all".

What about the connection: "exerts a strong influence"?

Premise 3 supports this with its phrases: "enforces" and "infuses them by a sort of enormous pressure." An influence is stronger where there is little or no defence against it, so Premise 2's "exposes him alone and unprotected to the influence of" certainly provides some further backing. And the element of defencelessness is reinforced by "he is instantly overwhelmed by the sense of his own insignificance and weakness" in Premise 1.

Taken together, the three premises provide reasonably strong support for the conclusion.

1. "The citizen consents to all the laws, even to those which are passed in spite of him, and even to those which punish him when he dares to violate any of them. The unvarying will of all the members of the State is the general will; it is through that that they are citizens and free. When a law is proposed in the assembly of the people, what is asked of them is not exactly whether they approve the proposition or reject it, but whether it is conformable or not with the general will, which is their own; each one in giving his vote expresses his opinion thereupon; and from the counting of the votes is obtained the declaration of the general will. When, therefore, the opinion opposed to my own prevails, that simply shows that I was mistaken, and that what I considered to be the general will was not so. Had my private opinion prevailed, I should have done something other than I wished; and in that case I should not have been free." J.-J. Rousseau, *The Social Contract*.

2. "Believe me, Sir, those who attempt to level, never equalize. In all societies, consisting of various descriptions of citizens, some description must be uppermost. The levellers, therefore, only change and pervert the natural order of things; they load the edifice of society by setting up in the air what the solidity of the structure requires to be on the ground." E. Burke, *Reflections on the Revolution in France*.

3. "It is part of the essence of judicial power to attend to private interests, and to fix itself with predilection on minute objects submitted to its observation; another essential quality of judicial power is never to volunteer its assistance to the oppressed, but always to be at the disposal of the humblest of those who solicit it; their complaint, however feeble they may themselves be, will force itself upon the ear of justice and claim redress, for this is inherent in

the very constitution of its courts of justice. A power of this kind is therefore peculiarly adapted to the wants of freedom, at a time when the eye and finger of government are constantly intruding into the minutest details of human actions, and when private persons are at once too weak to protect themselves, and too much isolated for them to reckon upon the assistance of their fellows." A. de Tocqueville, *Democracy in America*.

4. "The steady habit of correcting and completing his own opinions by collating it with those of others, so far from causing doubt and hesitation in carrying it into practice, is the only stable foundation for a just reliance on it; for, being cognizant of all that can, at least obviously, be said against him, and having taken up his position against all gain-sayers — knowing that he has sought for objections and difficulties instead of avoiding them, and has shut out no light which can be thrown upon the subject from any quarter — he has a right to think his judgement better than that of any person, or any multitude, who have not gone through a similar process." J.S. Mill, *On Liberty*.

5. "Labour is the fundamental basis of dignity and human rights, for it is only by means of his own free, intelligent work that man becomes a creator in his turn, wins from the surrounding world and his own animal nature his humanity and rights, and creates the world of civilization." M. Bakunin, *Principles and Organization of the International Brotherhood*.

6. "It is surely undeniable that, when a man engages in remunerative labour, the very reason and motive of his work is to obtain property, and to hold it as his own private possession. If one man hires out to another his strength or his industry, he does this for the purpose of receiving in

return what is necessary for food and living; he thereby expressly proposes to acquire a full and real right, not only to the remuneration, but also to the disposal of that remuneration as he pleases. Thus, if he lives sparingly, saves money, and invests his savings, for greater security, in land, the land in such a case is only his wages in another form; and, consequently, a working man's little estate thus purchased should be as completely at his own disposal as the wages he receives for his labour. But it is precisely in this power of disposal that ownership consists, whether the property be land or movable goods. The Socialists, therefore, in endeavouring to transfer the possessions of the individuals to the community, strike at the interests of every wage earner, for they deprive him of the liberty of disposing of his wages, and thus of all hope and possibility of increasing his stock and of bettering his condition in life." Pope Leo XIII, *Rerum Novarum*.

7. "To be a capitalist is to have not only a purely personal, but a social status in production. Capital is a collective product, and only by the united action of many members, nay, in the last resort, only by the united action of all members of society, can it be set in motion. Capital is therefore not a personal, it is a social power." K. Marx & F. Engels, *The Communist Manifesto*.

8. "Once you think about the point that not all wickedness is aggression, it may seem obvious. A great deal of the harm done in the world is plainly done from motives which are negative, which stop people from doing things which they ought to do. If, therefore, we are asking about the innateness of bad motives, we have to consider these other motives as well as aggression. For instance, sloth, fear, greed, and habit account for an enormous amount of ill-doing. Because people need each other's help so badly, these

negative motives can do almost infinite harm." Mary Midgley, *Wickedness*. Reprinted with permission, Routledge.

9. "Anyone who has ever learned a foreign language knows that the study of its vocabulary alone will not make him master of the new tongue. Even if he were to memorize a whole dictionary, he would not be able to make the simplest statement correctly; for he could not form a sentence without certain *principles of grammar*. He must know that some words are nouns and some are verbs; he must recognize some as active or passive forms of verbs, and know the person and number they express; he must know where the verb stands in the sentence in order to make the sense he has in mind. Mere separate names of things (even of actions, which are 'named' by infinitives) do not constitute a sentence. A string of words which we might derive by running our eye down the left-hand column in the dictionary—for instance 'especially espouse espringal espry esquire'—does not *say* anything. Each word has meaning, yet the series of words has none. Grammatical structure, then, is a further source of significance." Suzanne Langer, *Philosophy in a New Key*. Reprinted with permission, Harvard University Press.

10. "The notion of obligation comes before that of rights, which is subordinate and relative to the former. A right is not effectual by itself, but only in relation to the obligation to which it corresponds, the effective exercise of a right springing not from the individual who possesses it, but from other men who consider themselves as being under a certain obligation toward him. Recognition of an obligation makes it effectual. An obligation which goes unrecognized by anybody loses none of the full force of its existence. A

right which goes unrecognized by anybody is not worth very much." Simone Weil, *The Need for Roots*.

11. "The idols and false notions which are now in possession of the human understanding, and have taken deep root therein, not only so beset men's minds that truth can hardly find entrance, but even after entrance is obtained, they will again in the very instauration of the sciences meet and trouble us, unless men being forwarned of the danger fortify themselves as far as may be against their assaults.... There are also Idols formed by the intercourse and association of men with each other, which I call Idols of the Market Place, on account of the commerce and consort of men there. For it is by discourse that men associate, and words are imposed according to the apprehension of the vulgar. Therefore the ill and unfit choice of words wonderfully obstructs the understanding." Francis Bacon, *Novum Organum*.